THE
ONE POT
STUDENT
COOKBOOK

THE
ONE POT
STUDENT
COOKBOOK

Bounty
Books

rhubarb &
ginger slump

An Hachette UK Company
www.hachette.co.uk

First published in Great Britain in 2017 by Spruce,
a division of Octopus Publishing Group Ltd,
Carmelite House, 50 Victoria Embankment,
London EC4Y 0DZ
www.octopusbooks.co.uk

This edition published in 2018 by Bounty Books,
a division of Octopus Publishing Group Ltd

ISBN 978-0-7537-3299-1

A CIP catalogue record for this book is available from the British Library

Printed and bound in China

10 9 8 7 6 5 4 3 2 1

Standard level spoon measurement are used in all recipes.
1 tablespoon = one 15 ml spoon
1 teaspoon = one 5 ml spoon

Both imperial and metric measurements have been given in all recipes. Use one set of measurements
only and not a mixture of both.

Ovens should be preheated to the specific temperature – if using a fan-assisted oven, follow
manufacturer's instructions for adjusting the time and the temperature.

Pepper should be freshly ground black pepper unless otherwise stated.

For the Bounty edition
Publisher: Lucy Pessell
Designer: Lisa Layton
Editor: Sarah Vaughan
Production Controller: Allison Gonsalves

contents

Introduction

When you move out of home for the first time, hopefully you will have gleaned enough skills to enable you to wash your own clothes, find your way around campus and cook yourself a decent meal. That doesn't mean you need to have perfected the culinary arts but being able to rustle up a passable dinner and expand your repertoire beyond toast and cereal will make mealtimes far more enjoyable.

Cooking everything in one dish is less daunting than having to master a number of different skills and, even if you don't have much experience in the kitchen beyond boiling the kettle or slicing cheese for sandwiches, you should soon be able to create a variety of healthy and tasty meals that will help to keep your limited budget in check. One-pot cooking minimizes preparation time and washing up, which is good news for anyone who doesn't want to spend hours in the kitchen but still wants to enjoy a home-cooked meal in the evening. It also reduces waste, as many recipes are adaptable – particularly stews and casseroles where you can chuck in any old vegetables and herbs that happen to be lying around, rather than consigning them to the food bin. One-pot cooking also conserves energy because you're not using every ring on the hob, or keeping the oven and hob running together for lengthy periods of time. Plus, a slow cooker uses less energy than a conventional electric oven, even when it has been on for 6 or 7 hours.

Kitchen equipment

Whether you're moving into student accommodation or a shared house, you'll need to bring a certain amount of utensils and equipment with you in order to prepare and cook food. It makes sense to put together a list of what you'll need and divide it up between you and your housemates before moving-in day. That way, you won't end up with a cupboard full of lemon squeezers and garlic crushers but only enough plates and cutlery for two people to eat dinner together. It's unlikely that you'll be able to afford to splash out on fancy gadgets and designer crockery and there's really no need – between wear and tear, accidents and neglect, the contents of a student kitchen will be put through their paces. However, one-pot cooking means you'll be relying on a large pan, casserole dish and probably another oven-to-table pot – and it's worth spending a little more to buy a couple of pieces of quality cookware that will stay the distance.

Essential utensils & equipment

Sharp knives Two good knives should cover all your needs – a large one for meat and fish and a smaller one for paring and cutting vegetables.

Utensils Measuring jug, two mixing bowls, wooden spoon, rolling pin, grater, spatula, chopping board, vegetable peeler, whisk, colander.

Hand-held blender You can buy a hand-held blender for a few pounds and you'll find this really useful for making soups and sauces.

SLOW COOKER

A number of the recipes in this book are prepared and cooked in a slow cooker. It's worth investing in one as you can use it to cook healthy, hearty meals with the minimum of effort. And if you thought slow cookers were all about casseroles, think again – you can prepare everything from pot-roast chicken to curry and even sponge puddings in them, so they're extremely versatile.

You can buy a good-quality, large-capacity slow cooker for under £30, which is great value, considering the time and money you'll save once you get into the habit of using it regularly.

Choose a brand name that you trust and check out online reviews before you decide which one to buy. If you're planning on cooking meals for your housemates, or you want to make extra portions to freeze, then size matters – choose a slow cooker with a capacity of 5–6 litres (5–6 quarts). It's also worth checking that it includes a timer, so it will stop cooking and just keep the food warm if you're away from home.

SLOW COOKER TIPS

Clean the cooker as soon as possible after use so food doesn't dry solid. Always unplug the slow cooker before cleaning it.

Don't add extra liquid to the cooker, unless stated in the recipe. The tight-fitting lid stops any liquid from evaporating so the food will stay moist.

Keep the lid on during cooking – it might be tempting to take a quick peek inside but you'll tamper with the temperature if you do.

Brown meat in a frying pan before adding it to the slow cooker. Okay, so that's not technically one-pot cooking but it's all in the name of flavour.

Storecupboard

One-pot cookery is perfectly suited to long and slow cooking and you'll need a cupboard full of healthy grains and pulses, as well as a good selection of fresh ingredients, plus herbs and spices to add depth of flavour to your meals.

Salt and pepper Fine salt and ground pepper are ideal for seasoning dishes, while sea salt and freshly ground pepper make a sophisticated addition to the dinner table.

Oil Vegetable oil is a good everyday option for cooking and olive oil is perfect for salad dressings, marinades and sauces.

Canned chopped tomatoes Essential for sauces, soups and stews, this is a cheap and nutritious ingredient that you can buy in bulk.

Onions and garlic These two ingredients are essential in many cuisines and they form the base for a lot of savoury dishes in this book. Make sure you have a steady supply of both onions and garlic in the kitchen.

Rice There are lots of different varieties of rice. You'll need arborio rice if you want to cook risottos and jasmine rice for Thai food. Brown rice is the healthy option but it takes longer to cook so take this into account when you're planning your meals. Pick a couple of the rice varieties that you think you'll use most often and buy in bulk.

Pasta Again, choose just a couple of large packets of the pasta shapes you think you will use most frequently so you don't end up with dozens of different types of pasta filling up your cupboard. Pasta is a student staple and is well suited to one-pot cooking so you'll be eating a lot of it.

Cans of beans Stock up on cheap, protein-rich varieties like kidney beans (great for chillies), borlotti and butter beans (ideal for adding bulk to soups) and chickpeas (perfect for stews, curries and salads).

Lentils Healthy, nutritious and incredibly cheap, what's not to like about lentils? Red lentils break down when they are cooked for a long time, which makes them really useful for thickening up soups and stews. French Puy lentils hold their shape and are delicious in confits and casseroles.

Meal planning & shopping lists

You'll save a lot of money on your food bill if you plan your meals in advance. By shopping for exactly what you need for each meal, you'll reduce food wastage and avoid costly impulse buys. It only takes a few minutes to work out a rough plan for the week's meals. Cooking together as a household will also save money but it does mean that you'll need to be a bit more organized and get everyone together to agree on the weekly meal plan, cooking rota and food shop.

Don't worry if you can't stick to the plan rigidly – things will crop up during the week, which means people heading out at the last minute, or bringing friends home for dinner. Luckily, one-pot cooking is pretty flexible when it comes to working around a student lifestyle and an extra person at the dinner table shouldn't put a spanner in the works. Likewise, one less for dinner simply means an extra portion that you can store in the fridge or freezer to be eaten another time.

Once you've worked out a rough plan for the week, it makes sense to do one large supermarket shop for all the main ingredients, plus other essentials that you'll need like milk, bread, cereal and fruit. If you don't have a car and don't fancy heaving a week's worth of food for a house full of hungry students on the bus, then online shopping is definitely the most convenient way to buy your groceries. Inevitably, there'll be extras required during the week and a little blackboard or notebook in the kitchen is a handy way to keep track of what's needed. That way, whoever is passing the shops can top up when they go out.

Variety is the spice of life

When you're planning your meals, take into account any dietary requirements, likes and dislikes so that everyone has a say in the week's menu. Alternatively, if there is a mix of vegetarians and meat-eaters, it might make more sense to prepare different meals. However you organize the cooking and planning, try to include a good variety of meals to keep dinnertime interesting. So, for example:

Monday: casserole – try the Mixed Seafood Casserole (page 125) or the Mustardy Squash, Carrot & Sweet Potato Casserole (page 129).

Tuesday: rice dish – try the Bacon, Pea & Courgette Risotto (page 80) or Pork & Tomato Rice Pot (page 112).

Wednesday: veggie meal – try the Veggie Bean Chilli (page 97) or Courgette and Herb Risotto (page 134).

Thursday: Italian night – try the Pizza Fiorentina (page 46) or Chicken, Butternut Squash and Goats' Cheese Pasta (page 66).

Friday: fish supper – try the Crispy Fish Pie (page 119) or Baked Seafood with Paprika (page 145).

Saturday: curry – try the Pea & Lamb Korma (page 118) or Green Veg Curry (page 100).

Sunday: meat lover's Sunday lunch – try the Roast Chicken with Butternut Squash (page 66) or Mediterranean Pork Stew (page 73).

Eat Well For Less

It's the age-old student conundrum – how do you eat well on a meagre budget that is already taking the strain of other important commitments like beer, gig nights ... oh, and books. Well luckily, one-pot meals are perfectly suited to upcycling humble everyday fare into incredible dishes that will please your wallet and your taste buds. And, when you do find you have a few spare pennies in your purse, you can splash out on more extravagant ingredients for special occasions.

Budget

Before you can start planning what you're going to cook and eat, you need to be aware of exactly how much you have to spend on food. That means looking at your total income and taking off the cost of your rent, bills and other recurring overheads and seeing what's left. You can do this on a monthly or weekly basis and either set aside a specific amount for food, or you can decide each week what you can realistically spend.

Next, you need to decide if you're shopping individually, or clubbing together with your housemates. The good thing about buying your food together is that you can take advantage of bulk buys and discounts; the downside is that the kitchen cupboards can end up becoming a bit of a free-for-all, and you won't have exclusive ownership rights to the last slab of cheese or your favourite box of cereal.

Don't be tempted by unrealistic offers – will you really work your way through two punnets of peaches in a day?

Pick up bargains at the end of the day and tuck them away in your freezer – this is a great option for meat and fish, which can be expensive.

Don't be afraid to shop around and buy different ingredients from different shops or market stalls.

Nothing beats a Saturday take-out curry or Chinese meal but with a little practice and not much effort you can make your own versions for a fraction of the cost.

shop

Once you've worked out your budget and food sharing arrangements, it's time to work out where you can get the most for your money. If you have more than one supermarket close by, you can try price comparison websites to ensure you're paying the cheapest price for your regular items. Many town centres have fruit and veg stalls and these can offer very good value for money. Plus, if you loiter around the stalls towards the end of the day, you'll find vendors offering massive discounts to clear their stock. Likewise, farmers' markets are worth a trip for good-quality seasonal produce. Online shopping can save you time and money – many supermarkets offer free delivery slots at unpopular times (which can work to your advantage as a student).

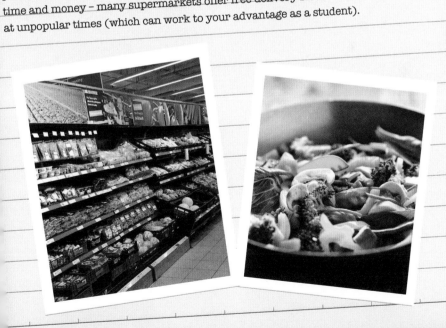

One-pot Entertaining

Entertaining at home doesn't have to entail long days sweating in the kitchen, arranging napkins into intricate shapes and trying to rustle up a matching 64-piece bone china dinner service. You can make it as laid back and low key as you like – after all, many students survive college on a diet of beans on toast, caffeine and alcohol so no one is going to judge your cooking or hosting skills too harshly. However, you probably want everyone to enjoy the meal so it's a good idea not to attempt a brand new recipe when you're entertaining eight people. Choose something you've made before and are confident cooking; that way you can relax and enjoy the evening too.

One-pot entertaining has a number of obvious benefits – less clutter on the worktops, less washing up and much less chance of spectacular failure. It's harder to overcook or burn a one-pot meal, as you just have the one dish to think about, plus you tend to add all – or most of – the ingredients at the same time, so there's less chance of forgetting something vital and spoiling the meal.

Don't forget to check if anyone is vegetarian: if they are, you'll need to decide whether to cook a meat-free meal or cook something different for your veggie mates. Likewise, if anyone has food allergies, intolerances – or is just plain fussy – it's better to find out before you're about to serve dinner.

Prep & cook times

You'll need to have some idea how long it will be until dinner's on the table, so each recipe is marked with a handy symbol:

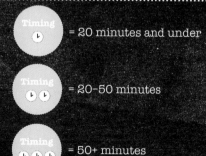

Timing = 20 minutes and under

Timing = 20–50 minutes

Timing = 50+ minutes

Top tips for a top night

- Plan ahead – check the timings for preparation and cooking and make sure you have the right amount of each ingredient.
- Buy a few nibbles to serve as a starter, to take the pressure off when cooking.
- Don't forget to preheat the oven so it's at the right temperature when you're ready to start cooking.
- Are you serving sides or bread with the meal? Don't forget to prepare these so they're ready at the same time as the main course.
- Check meat and fish are cooked through thoroughly before serving – you don't want to give your mates food poisoning.
- Create a playlist for the evening. That way, you won't have to get up and change the music in the middle of the meal.
- Check you have enough plates, cutlery and glasses well in advance.
- If you only have a small fridge, use a cool box and some ice packs for storing drinks – reserve fridge space for the food.

How to use this book

Each recipe in the book can be prepared and cooked in just one dish – whether that's a slow cooker, casserole dish, saucepan, ovenproof dish or a bowl in the microwave. There is also a number of cold dishes and salads that don't require any cooking at all – all you have to do is mix the ingredients together and serve.

In addition to the one dish, you will also need a few basic kitchen utensils to cook the recipes (see Essential Utensils & Equipment, page 7), and occasionally a recipe will call for a kitchen appliance, such as a microwave or slow cooker.

Most of the ingredients you need are everyday items that are not costly or difficult to source, though we have included a few more unusual recipes for special occasions and for when you become more confident and creative in the kitchen.

To help you keep within your food budget, each recipe in this book is rated with the below money symbols, indicating an approximate amount of how much each dish will cost you to make:

Cost £	Cost ££	Cost £££
Cheap, end-of-term saviours.	Spend a little more for some extra ingredients.	Splash out and impress all your friends.

what's for lunch?

chicken sweetcorn
chowder

rösti with smoked
salmon & rocket salad

feel-good broth

- 2 boneless, skinless chicken breasts, about 300 g (10 oz) in total
- 900 ml (1½ pints) cold chicken stock (see page 109 for homemade)
- 1 lemon slice
- 2 teaspoons roughly chopped thyme
- 250 g (8 oz) fresh meat cappelletti or small tortellini
- salt and pepper
- grated Parmesan cheese, to serve

what you do

1. Put the chicken breasts, stock, lemon slice and thyme in a large saucepan. Bring to a very gentle simmer – the water should shiver rather than bubble in the pan. Cover and cook for 15–16 minutes until the chicken is opaque all the way through. Remove and discard the lemon slice.
2. Lift the chicken from the liquid with a slotted spoon and transfer to a plate. When the chicken is cool enough to handle, shred into large pieces.
3. Bring the stock to a rapid boil and season with salt and pepper. Add the pasta and cook for 2–3 minutes, adding the shredded chicken for the last minute of the cooking time. Serve immediately with a generous scattering of grated Parmesan.

chicken mulligatawny

what You do

1. Melt half the butter in a saucepan and fry the chicken thighs in two batches for 5 minutes each, until golden on all sides. Lift out with a slotted spoon on to a plate.
2. Add the remaining butter and fry the onions, carrots and apple, stirring, for 6–8 minutes, until lightly browned.
3. Sprinkle in the flour and cook, stirring, for 1 minute. Gradually blend in the stock, then stir in the curry paste, tomato purée and rice. Return the chicken to the pan and bring to a simmer, stirring. Reduce the heat, cover and gently cook for 1 hour, or until the chicken is cooked through and very tender.
4. Lift the chicken from the soup with a slotted spoon and transfer to a plate. Once cool enough, pull the meat from the bones. Shred half the meat into pieces and return the remainder to the pan. Blend the soup using a hand-held blender.
5. Return the shredded chicken to the pan and heat through. Season to taste with salt and pepper. Ladle the soup into bowls and serve topped with spoonfuls of yogurt.

what You need

- 50 g (2 oz) butter
- 600 g (1 lb 3 oz) bone-in, skinless chicken thighs
- 2 onions, chopped
- 2 small carrots, chopped
- 1 small cooking apple, peeled, cored and chopped
- 1 tablespoon plain flour
- 1 litre (1¾ pints) chicken stock (see page 109 for homemade)
- 2 tablespoons mild curry paste
- 2 tablespoons tomato purée
- 50 g (2 oz) basmati rice
- salt and pepper
- natural yogurt, to serve

spicy chicken soup with avocado

Cost	Timing	Serves
£ £		4

what You do

what You need

- 2 tablespoons olive oil
- 1 onion, chopped
- 3 garlic cloves, crushed
- 1 teaspoon chipotle peppers in adobo sauce, chopped, or Tabasco sauce
- 2 teaspoons sugar
- 400 g (13 oz) can chopped tomatoes
- 1 litre (1¾ pints) hot chicken stock (see page 109 for homemade)
- 2 ready-cooked chicken breasts, torn into strips
- 1 ripe avocado, peeled, stoned and cubed
- handful of tortilla chips, crushed
- 4 tablespoons soured cream
- handful of chopped fresh coriander
- salt and pepper

1. Heat the oil in a large saucepan. Add the onion and cook for 5 minutes until softened, then stir in the garlic, chipotle peppers or Tabasco sauce and sugar. Pour in the tomatoes and stock, bring to the boil, then reduce the heat and simmer for 10 minutes.

2. Use a hand-held blender to purée the soup until smooth, then add a little boiling water if it is too thick and season to taste with salt and pepper.

3. Ladle the soup into serving bowls and scatter the chicken, avocado and tortilla chips on top. Drizzle with the soured cream and sprinkle with the chopped coriander.

Cooking tip
The fresh coriander adds another burst of flavour to the curry. To save wasting the rest of the pack, roughly chop the coriander and freeze in a small polythene bag for another time.

chicken sweetcorn chowder

Cost £

Timing ⏱

Serves 4

what you need

- 325 g (11 oz) can creamed sweetcorn
- 450 ml (¾ pint) milk
- 175 g (6 oz) ready-cooked chicken, torn into pieces
- 125 g (4 oz) frozen sweetcorn kernels
- 2 spring onions, chopped
- 2 teaspoons cornflour
- salt and pepper
- crusty bread, to serve

what you do

1. Place the creamed sweetcorn in a saucepan with the milk and heat, stirring.
2. Add the chicken, sweetcorn kernels and spring onions and season with salt and pepper. Simmer for 5 minutes, stirring occasionally.
3. Blend the cornflour with 1 tablespoon water in a mug, pour into the soup and stir to thicken. Ladle the soup into serving bowls and serve with crusty bread.

masala dhal & sweet potato

Cost £ **Timing** ⏱⏱⏱ **Serves** 4

what you do

1. Heat the oil in a saucepan and fry the onions for 5 minutes. Add the garlic, chilli flakes, ginger, garam masala and turmeric and cook, stirring, for 2 minutes.
2. Add the split peas, tomatoes and 750 ml (1¼ pints) of the stock and bring to the boil. Reduce the heat, cover and cook gently for 20 minutes, or until the peas have started to soften, adding more stock if the mixture runs dry.
3. Stir in the sweet potatoes, re-cover and cook for a further 20 minutes, or until the potatoes and peas are tender, adding more stock if necessary to keep the dhal juicy. Tip the spinach into the pan and stir until wilted. Add a little salt to taste. Serve with warm naan breads and mango chutney.

what you need

- 3 tablespoons vegetable oil
- 2 onions, chopped
- 2 garlic cloves, crushed
- ½ teaspoon dried red chilli flakes
- 1.5 cm (¾ inch) piece of fresh root ginger, peeled and grated
- 2 teaspoons garam masala
- ½ teaspoon ground turmeric
- 250 g (8 oz) dried split yellow peas, rinsed and drained
- 200 g (7 oz) can chopped tomatoes
- 1 litre (1¾ pints) vegetable stock (see page 34 for homemade)
- 500 g (1 lb) sweet potatoes, scrubbed and cut into small chunks
- 200 g (7 oz) spinach, washed and drained
- salt

To serve
- warm naan breads
- mango chutney

chickpea & red pepper soup

Cost
£

Timing

Serves
4

- 2 tablespoons olive oil
- 1 onion, finely chopped
- 1 red pepper, cored, deseeded and chopped
- 2 garlic cloves, crushed
- 2 teaspoons tomato purée
- 1 teaspoon ground cumin
- ½ teaspoon ground coriander
- pinch of cayenne pepper
- pinch of saffron threads
- 1.5 litres (2½ pints) hot vegetable stock (see page 34 for homemade)
- 400 g (13 oz) can chickpeas, rinsed and drained
- 125 g (4 oz) couscous
- finely grated zest and juice of 1 lemon
- salt and pepper

To garnish
- handful of chopped mint
- handful of chopped fresh coriander

what you do

1. Heat the oil in a large heavy-based saucepan. Add the onion and cook for 5 minutes, then add the red pepper, garlic, tomato purée and spices and cook for a further 1 minute.
2. Pour in the stock and bring to the boil, then reduce the heat and simmer for 5 minutes. Add the chickpeas and simmer for a further 5 minutes, then season to taste with salt and pepper.
3. Add the couscous and a squeeze of lemon juice and cook for 1 minute, or until the couscous is tender. Ladle into serving bowls and garnish with the chopped herbs and grated lemon zest.

pesto lemon soup

Cost
£

Timing

Serves
6

what You need

- 1 tablespoon olive oil
- 1 onion, finely chopped
- 2 garlic cloves, finely chopped
- 2 tomatoes, skinned (see cooking tip) and chopped
- 1.2 litres (2 pints) vegetable stock (see page 34 for homemade)
- 1 tablespoon shop-bought fresh green pesto, plus extra to serve
- grated zest and juice of 1 lemon
- 100 g (3½ oz) broccoli, cut into small florets and stems sliced
- 150 g (5 oz) courgettes, diced
- 100 g (3½ oz) frozen podded soya beans
- 65 g (2½ oz) small dried pasta shapes
- 50 g (2 oz) spinach, washed, drained and shredded
- salt and pepper
- basil leaves, to garnish (optional)
- olive or sun-dried tomato focaccia or ciabatta, to serve

what You do

1. Heat the oil in a saucepan and gently fry the onion for 5 minutes, or until softened. Add the garlic, tomatoes, stock, pesto, lemon zest and a little salt and pepper and simmer gently for 10 minutes.
2. Add the broccoli, courgettes, soya beans and pasta shapes and simmer for 6 minutes.
3. Stir the spinach and lemon juice into the pan and cook for 2 minutes, or until the spinach has just wilted and the pasta is just tender.
4. Ladle the soup into serving bowls, top with extra spoonfuls of pesto and garnish with a few basil leaves, if liked. Serve with olive or sun-dried tomato focaccia or ciabatta.

Cooking tip

Tomato skins don't soften, even when cooked for some time, so are worth removing. Pull away the stalks, make a slit with a knife and place the tomatoes in a heatproof bowl. Cover with boiling water and leave to stand for about 30 seconds if the tomatoes are very ripe, or a couple of minutes if very firm. Drain and fill the bowl with cold water. Peel away the skins and halve or chop the tomatoes as required.

minted pea soup

what you need

- 15 g (½ oz) butter
- 1 onion, finely chopped
- 1 potato, finely chopped
- 1 litre (1¾ pints) vegetable stock (see page 34 for homemade)
- 400 g (13 oz) frozen peas
- 6 tablespoons finely chopped mint, plus sprigs, to garnish
- salt and pepper
- crème fraîche (optional), to serve

what you do

1. Melt the butter in a saucepan, add the onion and potato and cook for 5 minutes. Pour in the stock and bring to the boil, then reduce the heat and simmer gently for 10 minutes, or until the potato is tender. Add the peas to the pan and cook for a further 3–4 minutes.
2. Season well with salt and pepper, then remove from the heat and stir in the mint. Blend the soup using a hand-held blender. Ladle into serving bowls and top each portion with a dollop of crème fraîche, if liked, some pepper and a mint sprig.

Variation
For a chunky pea and ham soup, cook 1 chopped carrot and 1 chopped turnip with the onion and potato, then add 1 litre (1¾ pints) chicken stock. Once the root vegetables are tender, add 300 g (10 oz) chopped ready-cooked ham, 4 finely chopped spring onions and 2 tablespoons chopped parsley with the peas and cook for 3–4 minutes. Do not blend the soup, but ladle into serving bowls and serve with crusty bread.

paella soup

what you need

Cost
££

Timing

Serves
4

- 1 tablespoon olive oil
- 1 onion, finely chopped
- 250 g (8 oz) chorizo sausage, chopped
- 2 garlic cloves, crushed
- 200 g (7 oz) can chopped tomatoes
- 1 litre (1¾ pints) chicken stock (see page 109 for homemade)
- pinch of saffron threads
- 2 skinless chicken breast fillets, cubed
- 1 red pepper, cored, deseeded and chopped
- 250 g (8 oz) ready-cooked rice
- 50 g (2 oz) frozen peas, defrosted
- salt and pepper

what you do

1. Heat the oil in a large heavy-based saucepan. Add the onion and chorizo and cook for 2 minutes, or until the onion has softened and the chorizo is lightly browned.
2. Stir in the garlic, then add the tomatoes, stock and saffron, and season to taste with salt and pepper. Bring to the boil, add the chicken and red pepper and simmer for 10–12 minutes or until the chicken is cooked through.

3. Add the rice and peas and cook for 2–3 minutes until heated through. Ladle the soup into serving bowls.

chorizo & black bean soup

Cost
£

Timing

Serves
4

what you need

- 2 tablespoons vegetable oil
- 1 onion, finely chopped
- 125 g (4 oz) chorizo sausage, finely diced
- 1 red pepper, cored, deseeded and chopped
- 1 garlic clove, chopped
- 1 teaspoon ground cumin
- 1.5 litres (2½ pints) hot chicken stock (see page 109 for homemade)
- 2 x 400 g (13 oz) cans black beans, rinsed and drained
- salt and pepper

To serve
- 2 tablespoons lime juice
- 4 tablespoons soured cream
- handful of chopped fresh coriander
- 1 red chilli, chopped

1. Heat the oil in a large heavy-based saucepan. Add the onion, chorizo, red pepper and garlic and cook for 7-10 minutes until softened, then stir in the cumin. Pour in the stock and beans and simmer for 5-8 minutes.
2. Season to taste with salt and pepper, then use a potato masher to roughly mash some of the beans to thicken the soup. Ladle the soup into serving bowls and sprinkle a little lime juice over each portion. Add a spoonful of soured cream, top with a sprinkling of the chopped coriander and chilli and serve immediately.

Varitation
For a chorizo and black bean salad, rinse and drain a 400 g (13 oz) can black beans. Put the beans in a bowl and mix with 2 tablespoons extra virgin olive oil and a good squeeze of lime juice. Season to taste with salt and pepper. Add 2 chopped tomatoes, 2 chopped spring onions and a good handful of chopped fresh coriander and toss to combine. Spoon the salad on to a serving plate and arrange slices of fried chorizo sausage on top. Serve with crusty bread.

wintery minestrone with pasta & beans

Cost **£**

Timing ◐ ◐

Serves **4**

what you need

- 2 tablespoons olive oil
- 1 onion, chopped
- 1 celery stick, chopped
- 1 carrot, chopped
- 1 garlic clove, crushed
- 400 g (13 oz) can chopped tomatoes
- 1.5 litres (2½ pints) vegetable stock (see page 34 for homemade)
- sprig of rosemary
- 150 g (5 oz) small soup pasta
- 75 g (3 oz) cavolo nero or other cabbage
- 200 g (7 oz) canned cannellini beans, rinsed and drained
- 4 tablespoons shop-bought fresh green pesto
- 25 g (1 oz) Parmesan cheese, grated
- salt and pepper
- crusty bread, to serve

what you do

1. Heat the oil in a large heavy-based saucepan. Add the onion, celery and carrot and cook for 5 minutes, or until softened, then add the garlic and cook for a further 1 minute.

2. Pour in the tomatoes and stock, add the rosemary and bring to the boil. Reduce the heat and simmer for 15 minutes.

3. Add the pasta and cabbage and cook for 5–7 minutes or according to the packet instructions. Stir in the beans and heat through, then season to taste with salt and pepper. Ladle the soup into serving bowls, drizzle with the pesto, sprinkle with the grated Parmesan and serve with crusty bread.

chicken, olive & cumin couscous

Cost
£

Timing
⏱

Serves
4

- 4 tablespoons olive oil
- rind and flesh of ½ lemon, finely chopped
- 1 tablespoon clear honey
- ½ teaspoon ground cumin
- 1 garlic clove, crushed
- 300 g (10 oz) couscous
- 300 ml (½ pint) hot chicken stock (see page 109 for homemade)
- 400 g (13 oz) can chickpeas, rinsed and drained
- 50 g (2 oz) green olives, pitted
- 2 ready-cooked chicken breasts, sliced
- handful each of chopped fresh coriander and mint, finely chopped
- salt and pepper

what you do

1. Heat the oil in a saucepan, add the lemon and cook over a gentle heat for about 2 minutes until the lemon is soft. Stir in the honey, cumin and garlic and heat through. Stir in the couscous, stock, chickpeas, olives and chicken.

2. Remove from the heat and leave to stand for 5 minutes, or until the couscous is tender. Fluff up the couscous with a fork and stir in the coriander and mint. Season to taste with salt and pepper and serve immediately.

balsamic roast veg salad

Cost £

Timing

Serves 4

what you need

- 1 red onion, roughly chopped
- 4 carrots, roughly chopped
- 1 red pepper, cored, deseeded and cut into large pieces
- 1 sweet potato, peeled and cut into even-sized pieces
- 400 g (13 oz) courgettes, peeled and cut into even-sized pieces
- 1 butternut squash, about 1 kg (2 lb), peeled, deseeded and cut into chunks
- 2 tablespoons olive oil, plus extra to drizzle
- 150 ml (¼ pint) balsamic vinegar
- 1 tablespoon chopped thyme
- 1 tablespoon chopped rosemary
- 75 g (3 oz) rocket
- salt and pepper

what you do

1. Put all the vegetables in a roasting tin, drizzle over the oil and balsamic vinegar and sprinkle with the herbs. Toss to make sure everything is well coated in the oil, then season to taste. Roast in a preheated oven, 190°C (375°F), Gas Mark 5, for 30 minutes, or until they are cooked and slightly crispy.
2. Remove the vegetables from the oven, allow to cool slightly, then toss with the rocket. Drizzle with olive oil, check the seasoning and serve.

STUDENT TIP

Student freezers are often filled with more ice than food. Don't wait until you can't shut the door: a regular defrost will help the freezer run more economically and maximize the storage space. This is a great revision-avoidance job.

greek salad with toasted pitta

what you need

Cost £ **Timing** ⏱ **Serves** 4

- 100 g (3½ oz) feta cheese, crumbled into smallish chunks
- 8–10 mint leaves, shredded
- 100 g (3½ oz) kalamata olives, pitted
- 2 tomatoes, chopped
- juice of 1 large lemon
- 1 small red onion, thinly sliced
- 1 teaspoon dried oregano
- 4 pitta breads
- lemon wedges, to serve

what you do

1. Toss together the feta, mint, olives, tomatoes, lemon juice, onion and oregano in a bowl.
2. Toast the pittas under a preheated hot grill until lightly golden, then split open and toast the open sides.
3. Tear the hot pittas into bite-sized pieces, then toss with the other salad ingredients in the bowl. Serve with lemon wedges.

Cooking tip

You'll find onions in many of the recipes in this book. If you want to chop them without ending up with red, watery eyes, try one of these tricks: chill them before chopping; chop them in a bowl of cold water; make sure your knife is super sharp for less exposure of cut areas; wear a swim mask when cutting them.

cauli cheese & leeks

what you need

Cost £   Timing   Serves 4

- 1 cauliflower, cut into florets
- 1 large leek, trimmed, cleaned and sliced
- 500 ml (17 fl oz) hot vegetable stock (see cooking tip for homemade)
- 2 tablespoons cornflour
- 150 ml (¼ pint) crème fraîche
- 100 g (3½ oz) Cheddar cheese, grated
- salt and pepper
- crusty bread, to serve

Cooking tip

For homemade vegetable stock, heat 1 tablespoon vegetable oil in a large saucepan and gently fry 2 unpeeled and roughly chopped onions, 2 each roughly chopped carrots, celery sticks, parsnips and courgettes and 200 g (7 oz) trimmed and sliced mushrooms, stirring frequently, for 10 minutes, or until softened. Add 3 bay leaves and a handful of parsley and thyme sprigs. Pour in 1.5 litres (2½ pints) cold water and bring to the boil. Reduce the heat and simmer very gently, uncovered, for 40 minutes. Strain through a sieve and leave to cool. Cover and store in the fridge for up to several days or freeze for up to 6 months.

what you do

1. Place the cauliflower and leek in a shallow flameproof casserole and pour in the stock. Cover and simmer for 5 minutes, then pour away half the stock.
2. Blend the cornflour with 3 tablespoons of the remaining stock in a mug, then stir in the crème fraîche. Pour the cornflour mixture into the casserole, add half the Cheddar and cook for 1 minute. Season to taste with salt and pepper.
3. Sprinkle the remaining Cheddar over the vegetables and place in a preheated oven, 200°C (400°F), Gas Mark 6, for 15-20 minutes until golden and bubbling. Serve with crusty bread.

chicken, lentils & kale

Cost £ Timing Serves 4

- 2 tablespoons olive oil
- 4 skinless chicken breast fillets
- 1 garlic clove, sliced
- 100 g (3½ oz) kale, tough stalks removed, and chopped
- 250 g (8 oz) can Puy lentils, rinsed and drained
- 2 tablespoons lemon juice
- 75 g (3 oz) sun-blush tomatoes
- 75 g (3 oz) soft goats' cheese, crumbled
- salt and pepper

what you do

1. Heat half the oil in a large frying pan with a lid. Add the chicken, season to taste with salt and pepper and cook for 5 minutes, then turn over and cook for a further 2 minutes, or until golden all over.
2. Add the remaining oil to the pan along with the garlic, kale and a splash of water. Cover and cook for 7 minutes, or until the kale is tender and the chicken cooked through.
3. Stir in the lentils and heat through, then add the lemon juice and tomatoes. Taste and adjust the seasoning if necessary.
4. Lift the chicken breasts from the pan with a slotted spoon and transfer to a plate. Cut the chicken into thick slices and arrange on serving plates with the lentils and kale. Scatter over the goats' cheese and serve immediately.

rösti with smoked salmon & rocket salad

Cost **££**

Timing

Serves **4**

what you need

- 750 g (1½ lb) waxy potatoes, coarsely grated
- 1 small onion, coarsely grated
- 50 g (2 oz) butter
- 3 tablespoons olive oil
- 2 tablespoons lemon juice
- 100 g (3½ oz) rocket
- salt and pepper

To serve
- 250 g (8 oz) smoked salmon
- lemon wedges

what you do

1. Place the potatoes and onion in a clean tea towel and squeeze to remove excess moisture. Season well with salt and pepper.
2. Heat the butter and 1 tablespoon of the oil in a nonstick frying pan. Tip in the potato mixture and spread out to make an even layer, then cook for about 10 minutes, or until the underside is golden. Invert the rösti on to a plate, then carefully slide it back into the pan to cook the other side. Cook for a further 5–8 minutes until cooked through and golden all over.
3. Meanwhile, make the rocket salad. Mix the lemon juice with the remaining oil in a bowl and toss with the rocket.
4. Cut the rösti into wedges and serve with the rocket salad, slices of smoked salmon and lemon wedges.

spicy mushrooms & cauli

 Cost
£

 Timing

 Serves
4

- 2 tablespoons sunflower oil
- 8 spring onions, cut into 5 cm (2 inch) lengths
- 2 teaspoons grated garlic
- 2 teaspoons ground ginger
- 2 tablespoons hot curry powder
- 200 g (7 oz) baby button mushrooms
- 300 g (10 oz) cauliflower florets
- 2 red peppers, cored, deseeded and cut into chunks
- 400 g (13 oz) can chopped tomatoes
- 200 g (7oz) canned chickpeas, rinsed and drained
- salt and pepper
- large handful of chopped mint, to garnish
- warm naan breads, to serve

what You do

1. Heat the oil in a large frying pan, add the spring onions and fry over a medium heat for 1–2 minutes.
2. Add the garlic, ginger and curry powder and fry, stirring, for 20–30 seconds until fragrant, then stir in the mushrooms, cauliflower and red peppers and fry for a further 2–3 minutes.
3. Stir in the tomatoes and bring to the boil. Reduce the heat to medium and simmer for 10–15 minutes, stirring occasionally. Add the chickpeas, season with salt and pepper and bring back to the boil. Garnish with the chopped mint and serve with warm naan breads.

caramelized parsnips

Cost £

Timing 🕐🕐

Serves 2

what you need

- 625 g (1¼ lb) parsnips, scrubbed or peeled
- 50 g (2 oz) butter
- 175 g (6 oz) diced bacon
- 3 tablespoons caster sugar
- 50 g (2 oz) pine nuts
- 5 tablespoons chopped thyme

what you do

1. Cut the parsnips in half widthways, then cut the chunky tops into quarters lengthways and the slim bottom halves in half lengthways.
2. Heat the butter in a large frying pan, add the bacon and parsnips and cook over a medium heat for about 15 minutes, turning and tossing occasionally, until the parsnips are golden and softened and the bacon is crisp.
3. Add the sugar and pine nuts and cook for a further 2–3 minutes until lightly caramelized. Toss with the thyme and serve.

STUDENT TIP

Even if you lack outdoor space you can still grow your own salad leaves and herbs — a few pots on the windowsill is all you need for a collection of fresh ingredients that will liven up pasta sauces, casseroles and salads for the price of a few packets of seeds.

flash-in-the-pan ratatouille

what you need

Cost
£

Timing

Serves
4

- 100 ml (3½ fl oz) olive oil
- 2 onions, chopped
- 1 aubergine, cut into 1.5 cm (¾ inch) cubes
- 2 large courgettes, cut into 1.5 cm (¾ inch) cubes
- 1 red pepper, cored, deseeded and cut into 1.5 cm (¾ inch) pieces
- 1 yellow pepper, cored, deseeded and cut into 1.5 cm (¾ inch) pieces

- 2 garlic cloves, crushed
- 400 g (13 oz) can chopped tomatoes
- 2–3 tablespoons balsamic vinegar
- 1 teaspoon soft brown sugar
- salt and pepper

To garnish
- 10–12 black olives, pitted
- basil leaves

what you do

1. Heat the oil in a large saucepan until very hot. Add all of the vegetables, except the tomatoes, and stir-fry for a few minutes.
2. Add the tomatoes, balsamic vinegar and sugar, season with salt and pepper and stir well. Cover tightly and simmer for 15 minutes, or until the vegetables are cooked.
3. Remove from the heat, scatter over the olives and basil leaves and serve immediately.

treacle & mustard beans

what you do

1. Put all the ingredients in a flameproof casserole and bring slowly to the boil, stirring occasionally.
2. Cover, transfer to a preheated oven, 160°C (325°F), Gas Mark 3, and bake for 1 hour. Remove the lid and bake for a further 30 minutes. Serve with garlic-rubbed bread.

what you need

- 1 carrot, diced
- 1 celery stick, chopped
- 1 onion, chopped
- 2 garlic cloves, crushed
- 2 x 400 g (13 oz) cans soya beans, drained
- 700 g (1 lb 7 oz) passata
- 75 g (3 oz) smoked bacon rashers, diced
- 2 tablespoons black treacle
- 2 teaspoons Dijon mustard
- salt and pepper
- garlic-rubbed bread (see tip), to serve

Accompaniment tip

For a garlic-rubbed bread, to serve as an accompaniment, heat a griddle pan until hot, add 6 thick slices of sourdough bread and cook for 2 minutes on each side until lightly charred. Rub each bread slice with a peeled garlic clove (or 2) and drizzle with extra virgin olive oil.

stir-fried veg rice

what you need

Cost	Timing	Serves
£	⏱ ⏱	4

- 2 tablespoons sunflower oil
- 6 spring onions, cut diagonally into 2.5 cm (1 inch) lengths
- 2 garlic cloves, crushed
- 1 teaspoon finely grated fresh root ginger
- 1 red pepper, cored, deseeded and finely chopped
- 1 carrot, finely diced
- 300 g (10 oz) peas
- 500 g (1 lb) ready-cooked long-grain rice
- 1 tablespoon dark soy sauce
- 1 tablespoon sweet chilli sauce
- chopped fresh coriander and mint, to garnish

what you do

1. Heat the oil in a large nonstick wok. Add the spring onions, garlic and ginger and stir-fry over a high heat for 4–5 minutes, then add the red pepper, carrot and peas and stir-fry for 3–4 minutes.
2. Stir in the rice and soy and sweet chilli sauces and stir-fry for 3–4 minutes until the rice is heated through and piping hot. Remove from the heat and serve immediately, garnished with the chopped herbs.

spinach & potato tortilla

Cost	Timing	Serves
£	🕐 🕐	4

- 3 tablespoons olive oil
- 2 onions, finely chopped
- 250 g (8 oz) ready-cooked potatoes, peeled and cut into 1 cm (½ inch) cubes
- 2 garlic cloves, finely chopped
- 200 g (7 oz) ready-cooked spinach, drained thoroughly and roughly chopped
- 4 tablespoons finely chopped ready-roasted red pepper
- 5 eggs, lightly beaten
- 3-4 tablespoons grated Manchego cheese
- salt and pepper

what you do

1. Heat the oil in an ovenproof, nonstick frying pan. Add the onions and potatoes and cook gently over a medium heat for 3-4 minutes, turning and stirring often, until the vegetables have softened but not coloured. Stir in the garlic, spinach and red pepper.
2. Season the eggs with salt and pepper, then pour them into the frying pan, shaking the pan so that the egg is evenly spread. Cook gently for 8-10 minutes until the tortilla is set at the bottom.
3. Sprinkle over the cheese. Place the frying pan under a preheated medium-hot grill and cook for 3-4 minutes until the top is set and golden.
4. Cut the tortilla into bite-sized squares or triangles and serve warm or at room temperature.

rtilla with tomato & rocket salad

at you need

ablespoons olive oil
nion, finely chopped
otatoes, thickly sliced
0 ml (7 fl oz) water
ggs, beaten

omato & rocket salad
5 g (3 oz) rocket
tablespoons extra virgin
live oil
tablespoons lemon juice
0 g (2 oz) sun-blush tomatoes
andful of Parmesan cheese
havings
alt and pepper

what you do

1 Heat the olive oil in an ovenproof nonstick frying pan. Add the onion and potato and cook for 5-10 minutes until golden, then pour in the measured water. Simmer gently until the potatoes are very tender, then carefully pour away any excess liquid.
2 Season the eggs with salt and pepper, then pour them into the pan and stir gently. Cook over a low heat for 10-15 minutes until set all the way through, finishing off under a preheated grill to set the top if necessary.
3 To make the salad, toss the rocket with the extra virgin olive oil, lemon juice and tomatoes in a bowl. Season well with salt and pepper and add the Parmesan shavings.
4 To serve, cut the tortilla into wedges and serve topped with the salad.

pan-cooked eggs

Cost
£

Timing
(clock)

Serves
2

what you need

- 25 g (1 oz) butter
- 1 leek, trimmed, cleaned and thinly sliced
- ½ teaspoon dried red chilli flakes
- 300 g (10 oz) baby spinach leaves
- 2 eggs
- 3 tablespoons natural yogurt
- pinch of paprika
- salt and pepper

what you do

1. Heat the butter in a frying pan, add the leek and chilli flakes and cook over a medium-high heat for 4–5 minutes until softened. Add the spinach and season well with salt and pepper, then toss and cook for 2 minutes until the spinach has wilted.

2. Make 2 hollows in the vegetables and break an egg into each hollow. Cook over a low heat for 2–3 minutes until the eggs are set. Spoon the yogurt on top and sprinkle with the paprika.

STUDENT TIP

Don't rely on corner shops and convenience stores for your groceries. Plan in advance and shop at larger supermarkets and food markets – your shopping will be much cheaper.

pizza fiorentina

Cost
£

Timing
▶

Serves
4

- 125 g (4 oz) baby spinach leaves
- 4 large wheat tortillas or flatbreads
- 150 ml (¼ pint) ready-made tomato sauce
- 125 g (4 oz) mozzarella cheese, sliced
- 4 eggs
- 25 g (1 oz) Parmesan cheese, grated

what you do

1. Place the spinach in a sieve and pour over boiling water from the kettle until it has wilted, then squeeze thoroughly to remove excess water.
2. Arrange the tortillas on 4 pizza trays. Spoon the tomato sauce over the tortillas, then scatter over the spinach and arrange the mozzarella on top. Crack an egg in the centre of each pizza.
3. Sprinkle the Parmesan over the pizzas, then place in a preheated oven, 220°C (425°F), Gas Mark 7, for 5–7 minutes until the egg whites are just set.

egg pots with smoked salmon

what you need

Cost	Timing	Serves
££	🕐	4

- butter, for greasing
- 200 g (7 oz) smoked salmon trimmings
- 2 tablespoons chopped chives
- 4 eggs
- 4 tablespoons double cream
- pepper
- toasted bread, to serve

what you do

1. Grease 4 ramekins with butter. Divide the smoked salmon and chives among the prepared ramekins. Using the back of a spoon, make a small hollow in the top of the salmon in each ramekin. Break an egg into each hollow, sprinkle with a little pepper and spoon the cream over the top.
2. Put the ramekins in a roasting tin and half-fill the tin with boiling water. Bake in a preheated oven, 180°C (350°F), Gas Mark 4, for 10–15 minutes until the eggs have just set.
3. Remove from the oven and leave to cool for a few minutes, then serve with the toasted bread

courgette & ricotta bakes

what you need

Cost £ **Timing** **Serves** 4

- butter, for greasing
- 2 courgettes
- 100 g (3½ oz) fresh white breadcrumbs
- 250 g (8 oz) ricotta cheese
- 75 g (3 oz) Parmesan cheese, grated
- 2 eggs, beaten
- 1 garlic clove, crushed
- handful of chopped basil
- salt and pepper

what you do

1. Lightly grease 8 holes in a large muffin tin with butter. Use a vegetable peeler to make 16 long ribbons of courgette and set aside. Coarsely grate the remainder of the courgettes on to a clean tea towel and squeeze to remove excess moisture.
2. To make the filling, mix the grated courgette with the remaining ingredients in a bowl and season well with salt and pepper.
3. Arrange 2 courgette ribbons in a cross shape in each hole of the prepared muffin tin. Spoon in the filling and fold over the overhanging courgette ends. Place in a preheated oven, 190°C (375°F), Gas Mark 5, for 15–20 minutes until golden and cooked through. Turn out on to serving plates.

vegetable bolognese

Cost
££

Timing

Serves
2

what you need

- 1 tablespoon vegetable oil
- 1 onion, finely chopped
- 1 garlic clove, finely chopped
- 1 celery stick, finely chopped
- 1 carrot, finely chopped
- 75 g (3 oz) chestnut mushrooms, roughly chopped
- 1 tablespoon tomato purée
- 400 g (13 oz) can chopped tomatoes
- 250 ml (8 fl oz) red wine or vegetable stock (see page 34 for homemade)
- pinch of dried mixed herbs
- 1 teaspoon yeast extract
- 150 g (5 oz) textured vegetable protein (TVP)
- 2 tablespoons chopped parsley
- salt and pepper

To serve
- cooked spaghetti
- grated Parmesan cheese

what you do

1. Heat the oil in a large heavy-based saucepan. Add the onion, garlic, celery, carrot and mushrooms and cook over a medium heat, stirring frequently, for 5 minutes, or until softened. Add the tomato purée and cook, stirring, for a further 1 minute.

2. Pour in the tomatoes and wine or stock, then add the dried herbs, yeast extract and vegetable protein. Bring to the boil, then reduce the heat, cover and simmer for 30–40 minutes until the vegetable protein is tender.

3. Stir in the parsley and season well with salt and pepper. Divide the sauce between serving plates and serve immediately with cooked spaghetti and a scattering of grated Parmesan.

stuffed courgettes

- 4 courgettes
- 175 g (6 oz) plum tomatoes, chopped
- 200 g (7 oz) mozzarella cheese, grated
- 2 tablespoons shredded basil
- 25 g (1 oz) Parmesan cheese, grated
- salt and pepper

what you do

1. Slice the courgettes in half horizontally and then scoop out the middle of each one, reserving the flesh. Place the courgette halves, cut-side up, in a roasting tin and bake in a preheated oven, 200°C (400°F), Gas Mark 6, for 10 minutes.

2. Meanwhile, to make the filling, chop the reserved courgette flesh and mix it in a bowl with the tomatoes, mozzarella and basil. Season to taste with salt and pepper.

3. Remove the courgette halves from the oven and spoon the filling into each one. Sprinkle with the Parmesan and return to the oven for 15 minutes, or until golden.

baked mushrooms with goats' cheese & rocket

what you need

Cost £

Timing ⏱ ⏱

Serves 4

- 500 g (1 lb) new potatoes, halved
- 3 tablespoons olive oil
- 200 g (7 oz) portobello mushrooms
- 2 tablespoons chopped thyme
- 6 garlic cloves, unpeeled
- 50 g (2 oz) soft goats' cheese
- 125 g (4 oz) cherry tomatoes
- salt and pepper
- 25 g (1 oz) toasted pine nuts, to garnish
- 75 g (3 oz) rocket, to serve

what you do

1. Put the potatoes in a large roasting tin, drizzle over 2 tablespoons olive oil and toss to make sure the potatoes are well coated in oil. Bake in a preheated oven, 220°C (425°F), Gas Mark 7, for 15 minutes, turning once halfway through the cooking time.
2. Add the mushrooms, stem-side up, to the tin, scatter over the thyme and garlic, drizzle over the remaining oil and season well with salt and pepper. Place a little goats' cheese on top of each mushroom and return to the oven for a further 5 minutes.
3. Add the cherry tomatoes to the tin and return to the oven for 5 minutes more, or until the potatoes and mushrooms are cooked through. Garnish with the pine nuts and serve with the rocket.

Spicy paneer with tomatoes, peas & beans

Cost
£

Timing
▶ ▶

Serves
4

What you need

- tablespoons vegetable oil
- 0 g (8 oz) paneer, diced
- onion, finely chopped
- garlic cloves, chopped
- teaspoons finely grated fresh
- ot ginger
- teaspoon ground coriander
- teaspoon paprika
- teaspoon tomato purée
- 25 ml (4 fl oz) hot vegetable
- stock (see page 34 for
- homemade)
- 150 g (5 oz) French beans,
- opped and tailed
- 75 g (6 oz) frozen peas
- 150 g (5 oz) tomatoes, chopped
- 1 teaspoon garam masala
- salt and pepper
- chapattis, to serve

what you do

1. Heat half the oil in a large frying pan with a lid. Add the paneer, season well with salt and pepper and cook for 3–4 minutes until golden all over. Lift out with a slotted spoon on to a plate.
2. Add the remaining oil and the onion to the pan and cook for 5 minutes, until softened. Stir in the garlic and ginger and cook for a further 1 minute, then add the spices and cook for 30 seconds.
3. Stir in the tomato purée and stock, then add the beans and return the paneer to the pan. Season to taste with salt and pepper, cover and simmer for 5 minutes.
4. Add the peas and tomatoes and cook for a further 3 minutes, then stir in the garam masala. Divide among serving bowls and serve with chapattis.

okra & coconut stew

Cost
£

Timing

Serves
3–4

what you need

- 375 g (12 oz) okra
- 4 tablespoons vegetable oil
- 2 onions, chopped
- 2 green peppers, cored, deseeded and cut into chunks
- 3 celery sticks, thinly sliced
- 3 garlic cloves, crushed
- 4 teaspoons Cajun spice blend
- ½ teaspoon ground turmeric
- 300 ml (½ pint) vegetable stock (see page 34 for homemade)
- 400 ml (14 fl oz) can coconut milk
- 200 g (7 oz) frozen sweetcorn
- juice of 1 lime
- 4 tablespoons chopped fresh coriander
- salt and pepper

what you do

1. Trim the stalk ends from the okra and cut the pods into 1.5 cm (¾ inch) lengths.
2. Heat 2 tablespoons of the oil in a large, deep-sided frying pan with a lid or shallow flameproof casserole and fry the okra for 5 minutes. Lift out with a slotted spoon on to a plate.
3. Add the remaining oil to the pan or casserole and very gently fry the onions, green peppers and celery, stirring frequently, for 10 minutes, or until softened but not browned. Add the garlic, spice blend and turmeric and cook for 1 minute.
4. Pour in the stock and coconut milk and bring to the boil. Reduce the heat, cover and cook gently for 10 minutes. Return the okra to the pan with the sweetcorn, lime juice and coriander and cook for a further 10 minutes. Season to taste with salt and pepper and serve.

vegetable & tofu stir-fry

Cost £

Timing ⏱

Serves 4

what you need

- 3 tablespoons sunflower oil
- 300 g (10 oz) firm tofu, cubed
- 1 onion, sliced
- 2 carrots, sliced
- 150 g (5 oz) broccoli, broken into small florets and stalks sliced
- 1 red pepper, cored, deseeded and sliced
- 1 large courgette, sliced
- 150 g (5 oz) sugar snap peas
- 2 tablespoons soy sauce
- 2 tablespoons sweet chilli sauce
- 125 ml (4 fl oz) water

To garnish
- 2 red chillies, chopped
- basil leaves

what you do

1. Heat 1 tablespoon of the oil in a wok until starting to smoke, add the tofu and stir-fry over a high heat for 2 minutes, or until golden. Lift out with a slotted spoon on to a plate.
2. Heat the remaining oil in the wok, add the onion and carrots and stir-fry for 1½ minutes. Add the broccoli and red pepper and stir-fry for 1 minute, then add the courgette and sugar snap peas and stir-fry for 1 minute.
3. Combine the soy and chilli sauces and the measured water in a mug, pour into the wok, then return the tofu to the wok and cook for 1 minute. Divide among serving bowls and garnish with the chopped red chillies and basil leaves.

Accompaniment Tip
For sesame noodles, to serve as an accompaniment, put 375 g (12 oz) egg thread noodles in a large heatproof bowl, pour over enough boiling water to cover and leave to stand for 4 minutes, or until just tender. Drain well, then toss with 1 tablespoon light soy sauce and 2 teaspoons sesame oil. Serve sprinkled with 1 tablespoon toasted sesame seeds.

spiced chickpeas & kale

what you need

Cost
£

Timing

Serves
4

- 3 tablespoons vegetable oil
- 3 red onions, cut into wedges
- 2 tablespoons mild curry paste
- 400 g (13 oz) can chopped tomatoes
- 400 g (13 oz) can chickpeas, rinsed and drained
- 300 ml (½ pint) vegetable stock (see page 34 for homemade)
- 2 teaspoons soft light brown sugar
- 100 g (3½ oz) kale, tough stalks removed
- salt and pepper

what you do

1. Heat the oil in a large saucepan and fry the onions for 5 minutes, or until beginning to colour. Stir in the curry paste and then the tomatoes, chickpeas, stock and sugar. Bring to the boil, then reduce the heat, cover and simmer gently for 20 minutes.

2. Stir in the kale and cook gently for a further 10 minutes. Season to taste with salt and pepper and serve.

tomato & basil tart

what you need

- butter for greasing
- 375 g (12 oz) ready-made puff pastry
- plain flour, for dusting
- 1 egg, beaten
- 200 g (7 oz) mascarpone cheese
- 50 g (2 oz) Parmesan cheese, grated
- handful of chopped basil, plus extra to garnish
- 150 g (5 oz) cherry tomatoes, halved
- 1 tablespoon olive oil
- salt and pepper

what you do

1. Lightly grease a baking sheet with butter. On a clean surface, lightly dusted with plain flour, roll out the pastry to a 30 cm (12 inch) disc. Place on the prepared baking sheet and roll the edges up to create a 1 cm (½ inch) border. Press the border down with your thumb to make a crumpled edge, then prick over the middle of the pastry disc a few times with a fork. Place in the freezer for a few minutes.

2. Brush the border of the pastry with a little of the beaten egg. Mix together the mascarpone, remaining egg, Parmesan and basil in a bowl, season to taste with salt and pepper and spread over the centre of the tart. Arrange the tomatoes on top of the tart and drizzle over the oil. Bake in a preheated oven, 220°C (425°F), Gas Mark 7, for 20–25 minutes until golden and crisp.

Mad About Mains

sausage & onion
traybake

paella

lemon chilli chicken

chicken, ham & cabbage stew

salmon with green vegetables

chicken with spring herbs

chicken, chorizo & black bean stew

roast chicken with butternut squash

chicken ratatouille

tandoori chicken & onions

chicken & tomato polenta pie

herby roast turkey breast

pork & leek stew

mediterranean pork stew

hoisin pork stir-fry

sausage & onion traybake

chorizo & chickpea stew

sweet & sour pork

liver & onions

bacon, pea & courgette risotto

spicy sausage & tomato

beef & pickled onion stew

beef & potato hash

beef goulash

west indian beef & bean stew

rustic lamb & potato curry

pollock & lentils

mackerel & sesame noodles

smoked haddock cannelloni

paella

baked cod with tomatoes & olives

roast sea bass with potatoes & mushrooms

spicy prawn & pea pilau

goats' cheese & pepper lasagne

veggie bean chilli

middle eastern courgette, tomato & mint curry

spicy green bean, potato & pesto linguini

green veg curry

ranch-style eggs

pesto puff tart

lemon chilli chicken

Cost ££

Timing

Serves 4

what you need

- 1 chicken, about 1.75 kg (3½ lb), jointed
- 8 garlic cloves, peeled
- 4 juicy lemons, quartered and squeezed, skins reserved
- 1 small red chilli, deseeded and chopped
- 2 tablespoons orange blossom honey
- 4 tablespoons chopped parsley, plus sprigs to garnish
- salt and pepper

what you do

Arrange the chicken pieces in a shallow, flameproof casserole. Crush 2 of the garlic cloves, then put them in a mug with the lemon juice, chilli and honey and stir well. Pour the mixture over the chicken. Tuck the lemon skins around the meat, cover with clingfilm and leave to marinate in the fridge for at least 2 hours or overnight, turning once or twice.

Turn the chicken pieces skin-side up, scatter over the remaining whole garlic cloves and place the lemon skins, cut-side down, on top. Cook the chicken in a preheated oven, 200°C (400°F), Gas Mark 6, for 45 minutes, or until golden brown, cooked through and tender. Stir in the parsley, season to taste with salt and pepper and serve garnished with sprigs of parsley.

chicken, ham & cabbage stew

Cost
££

Timing
🕐 🕐 🕐

Serves
6

- 150 g (5 oz) dried haricot beans, soaked in a bowl of cold water overnight
- 1 ham hock or gammon joint, about 750 g (1½ lb), soaked in a bowl of cold water overnight
- 4 chicken legs
- 2 onions, chopped
- 3 bay leaves
- 1.2 litres (2 pints) cold water
- 500 g (1 lb) floury potatoes
- 1 tablespoon paprika
- 200 g (7 oz) green cabbage, shredded
- 15 g (½ oz) fresh coriander, roughly chopped
- pepper

what you do

1. Drain the beans and transfer to a large saucepan. Cover with fresh cold water and bring to the boil. Reduce the heat and simmer for 40 minutes, or until just tender. Drain and set aside.
2. Add the drained ham to the empty bean pan with the chicken legs, onions and bay leaves. Pour over the measured water and bring to a gentle simmer. Cover and cook very gently for 1 hour.
3. Cut the potatoes into small chunks and add to the pan with the beans and paprika. Cook very gently, covered, for a further 20 minutes, or until the potatoes are tender.
4. Lift the chicken and ham from the pan with a slotted spoon and transfer to a plate. Once cool enough to handle, pull the meat from the bones, discarding the skin. Shred or chop all the meat into small pieces.
5. Return the meat to the pan. Stir in the cabbage and coriander and heat through gently. Season with pepper and serve.

lmon with green vegetables

Cost
£££

Timing
⏱ ⏱

Serves
4

what you need

1 tablespoon olive oil
1 leek, trimmed, cleaned and thinly sliced
275 ml (9 fl oz) fish stock (see page 125 for homemade)
200 ml (7 fl oz) crème fraîche
125 g (4 oz) frozen peas
125 g (4 oz) frozen soya or broad beans
4 chunky skinless salmon fillets, about 150 g (5 oz) each
2 tablespoons snipped chives
pepper
mashed potato, to serve

what you do

1. Heat the oil in a large heavy-based frying pan with a lid and cook the leek over a medium heat, stirring frequently, for 3 minutes, or until softened. Pour in the stock, bring to the boil and continue boiling for 2 minutes, or until reduced a little.
2. Add the crème fraîche and stir well to mix. Add the peas, soya or broad beans and salmon and return to the boil. Reduce the heat, cover and simmer for 10 minutes, or until the fish is opaque and cooked through and the peas and beans are piping hot.
3. Sprinkle over the chives, season with pepper and serve spooned over instant mashed potato.

STUDENT TIP

It's cheaper to buy a whole chicken and cut it into portions. You could ask the butcher to do this for you or, if you have a good-quality sharp knife, you could do it yourself. It's simply a case of cutting the chicken in half, then separating the legs from the breast and cutting the legs from the thighs — this will give you six portions ready for the pot.

chicken with spring herbs

what you need

- 250 g (8 oz) mascarpone cheese
- handful of chervil, finely chopped
- ½ bunch of parsley, finely chopped
- 2 tablespoons chopped mint

- 4 boneless, skin-on chicken breasts
- 25 g (1 oz) butter
- 200 ml (7 fl oz) white wine
- salt and pepper
- garlic bread, to serve (optional)

what you do

1. Mix together the mascarpone and herbs in a bowl and season well with salt and pepper. Lift the skin away from each chicken breast and spread a quarter of the mascarpone mixture on each breast. Replace the skin and smooth carefully over the mascarpone mixture. Season with salt and pepper.

2. Place the chicken breasts in a baking dish, dot with the butter and pour the wine around it. Roast the chicken in a preheated oven, 180°C (350°F), Gas Mark 4, for 20–25 minutes until golden and crisp and cooked through. Serve with garlic bread, if liked.

chicken, chorizo & black bean stew

what you need

- 250 g (8 oz) dried black beans, soaked in a bowl of cold water overnight
- 8 bone-in, skinless chicken thighs
- 150 g (5 oz) chorizo sausage, cut into small chunks
- 1 onion, sliced
- 1 fennel bulb, trimmed and chopped
- 2 green peppers, cored, deseeded and cut into chunks
- 1 teaspoon saffron threads
- salt and pepper

what you do

1. Drain the beans and transfer to a large flameproof casserole. Cover with plenty of fresh cold water. Bring to the boil and boil for 10 minutes. Drain the beans and return to the pan.
2. Add the chicken, chorizo, onion, fennel and green peppers and sprinkle in the saffron. Almost cover the ingredients with cold water and bring to a simmer. Cover and cook in a preheated oven, 160°C (325°F), Gas Mark 3, for 2 hours, or until the beans are very soft.
3. Using a slotted spoon, drain a couple of spoonfuls of the beans and transfer them to a bowl. Mash the beans with a fork and then return to the casserole, stirring gently to thicken the juices. Season to taste with salt and pepper and serve.

roast chicken with butternut squash

Cost
££

Timing

Serves
4

- 500 g (1 lb) butternut squash, peeled, deseeded and cut into thin slices
- 1 red onion, sliced
- 4 bone-in, skin-on chicken breasts
- 2 tablespoons olive oil
- 1 tablespoon balsamic vinegar
- 25 g (1 oz) walnut halves
- 8 sage leaves
- salt and pepper

To serve
- crusty bread
- green salad

Variation
For a chicken, butternut squash and goats' cheese pasta, cook 250 g (8 oz) peeled, deseeded and diced butternut squash in a large saucepan of lightly salted boiling water for 6 minutes. Add 500 g (1 lb) fresh penne pasta and cook for a further 3 minutes, or according to the packet instructions. Add 150 g (5 oz) baby spinach leaves, then drain immediately and return the pasta and vegetables to the pan. Stir in 75 g (3 oz) soft goats' cheese and 1 ready-cooked chicken breast, torn into shreds, then season to taste with salt and pepper and serve topped with roughly chopped walnuts.

what you do

1. Arrange the squash, onion and chicken in a roasting tin. Drizzle over the oil, season to taste with salt and pepper and toss to make sure everything is well coated in oil. Turn the chicken skin-side up and roast in a preheated oven, 200°C (400°F), Gas Mark 6, for 15 minutes.
2. Drizzle over the balsamic vinegar and scatter the walnuts and sage leaves around the chicken. Return to the oven for 5–10 minutes until the squash is tender and the chicken is cooked through. Serve with crusty bread and green salad.

chicken ratatouille

Cost
£

Timing

Serves
4

what You do

1. Cut a couple of slashes across each chicken thigh and season with salt and pepper. Heat the oil in a large, deep frying pan, add the chicken and cook over a high heat for 5 minutes, turning occasionally.
2. Add the onion, aubergine, green and red peppers, courgettes and garlic and cook for 10 minutes, or until softened, adding a little water if the mixture becomes too dry.
3. Pour in the tomatoes, add the sugar and season to taste with salt and pepper. Bring to the boil, stirring, then reduce the heat, cover and simmer for 15 minutes, stirring occasionally. Stir in the basil and serve.

what You need

- 8 small skinless chicken thighs
- 1 tablespoon olive oil
- 1 onion, chopped
- 1 aubergine, cut into bite-sized chunks
- 1 green pepper, cored, deseeded and cut into bite-sized chunks
- 1 red pepper, cored, deseeded and cut into bite-sized chunks
- 2 courgettes, chopped
- 1 garlic clove, crushed
- 400 g (13 oz) can chopped tomatoes
- pinch of caster sugar
- handful of basil leaves, roughly torn
- salt and pepper

tandoori chicken & onions

what you need

Cost ££   **Timing** 🕐🕐   **Serves** 4

- 4 skinless chicken breast fillets
- 100 ml (3½ fl oz) natural yogurt
- 1 garlic clove, crushed
- 2 teaspoons finely grated fresh root ginger
- 2 tablespoons tandoori curry paste
- 1 onion, cut into wedges
- 2 tablespoons vegetable oil

- 2 tomatoes, quartered
- 15 g (½ oz) butter, cut into small pieces
- salt and pepper

To serve
- lime wedges
- ready-made raita
- warm naan breads

what you do

1. Line a baking sheet with foil and set a wire rack on top. Make 3 slashes across each chicken breast. Mix together the yogurt, garlic, ginger and tandoori paste in a bowl and season well with salt and pepper. Add the chicken and rub the tandoori mixture all over the chicken. Leave to marinate for 5–10 minutes.

2. Toss the chicken with the onion and oil, then arrange on the rack. Bake in a preheated oven, 230°C (450°F), Gas Mark 8, for 7 minutes.

3. Add the tomatoes, scatter over the butter and return to the oven for a further 5–10 minutes until the chicken is charred and cooked through. Serve with lime wedges, raita and warm naan breads.

STUDENT TIP

Always label your freezer food clearly — unless you don't mind having a lucky dip dinner in a couple of weeks' time. Buy a batch of freezer bags, stickers and a suitable marker pen and keep them somewhere handy so you can batch up leftovers quickly.

chicken & tomato polenta pie

Cost
££

Timing

Serves
4

what you need

- 2 tablespoons olive oil
- 300 g (10 oz) skinless chicken breast fillets, diced
- 2 garlic cloves, finely chopped
- 400 g (13 oz) can chopped tomatoes
- 1 teaspoon tomato purée
- pinch of dried red chilli flakes
- handful of chopped basil
- 1 courgette, sliced
- 500 g (1 lb) ready-cooked polenta, cut into 1 cm (½ inch) slices
- 25 g (1 oz) Parmesan cheese, grated
- salt and pepper

what you do

1. Heat the oil in a shallow flameproof casserole. Add the chicken, season to taste with salt and pepper and cook for 3–4 minutes until starting to turn golden. Lift out with a slotted spoon on to a plate.
2. Add the garlic to the casserole and cook for 1 minute, then pour in the tomatoes and stir in the tomato purée, chilli flakes and basil. Bring to the boil, then reduce the heat and simmer for 10 minutes.
3. Return the chicken to the casserole, add the courgette and cook for a further 5–10 minutes until the chicken is cooked through.
4. Arrange the polenta slices on top of the chicken mixture, then scatter over the Parmesan. Cook under a preheated hot grill for 5 minutes, or until golden and bubbling.

herby roast turkey breast

what you need

Cost
£££

Timing

Serves
4

- handful of chopped rosemary
- handful of chopped parsley
- 25 g (1 oz) butter, softened
- 800 g (1 lb 10 oz) turkey breast joint
- 6 garlic cloves
- 50 ml (2 fl oz) dry white wine
- 50 ml (2 fl oz) hot chicken stock (see page 109 for homemade)
- 4 slices of pancetta
- 2 x 400 g (13 oz) cans butter beans, rinsed and drained
- handful of sun-blush tomatoes, roughly chopped
- 50 ml (2 fl oz) double cream
- salt and pepper

what you do

1. Mix together the rosemary, three-quarters of the parsley and the butter in a bowl. Smear the flavoured butter over the turkey joint. Season to taste with salt and pepper.
2. Place the turkey in a roasting tin with the whole garlic cloves, pour the wine and stock into the tin and arrange the pancetta on top of the turkey. Roast in a preheated oven, 220°C (425°F), Gas Mark 7, for 25 minutes.
3. Add the beans, tomatoes and cream to the roasting tin, topping up with a little water if necessary. Season to taste with salt and pepper, then return to the oven for a further 3–5 minutes until the turkey is cooked through and the beans are warm.
4. Cut the turkey into slices and arrange on serving plates with the crispy pancetta and the beans, sprinkled with the remaining parsley.

pork & leek stew

what you need

Cost
££

Timing
● ● ●

Serves
4–5

- 1 kg (2 lb) boneless lean pork, diced
- 2 tablespoons vegetable oil
- 1 large onion, chopped
- 500 g (1 lb) leeks, trimmed, cleaned and chopped
- 3 bay leaves
- 1.5 litres (2½ pints) chicken or beef stock (see pages 109 or 84 for homemade)

- 75 g (3 oz) pearl barley
- 150 g (5 oz) self-raising flour
- 75 g (3 oz) beef or vegetable suet
- about 125 ml (4 fl oz) cold water
- 150 g (5 oz) stoned prunes, halved
- salt and pepper

what you do

1. Season the pork with plenty of salt and pepper. Heat 1 tablespoon of the oil in a large flameproof casserole and fry the pork in batches until browned on all sides, lifting out with a slotted spoon on to a plate.
2. Add the remaining oil to the casserole and gently fry the onion and leeks for 5 minutes. Return the pork to the casserole, add the bay leaves and stock and bring to a simmer. Stir in the pearl barley. Cover, reduce the heat to its lowest setting and cook for about 1½ hours until the pork and barley are tender and the cooking juices have thickened.
3. Mix together the flour, suet and a little salt and pepper in a bowl. Add the measured water and mix with a round-bladed knife to a soft dough, adding a dash more water if the mixture feels dry and crumbly, but don't make it too sticky.
4. Stir the prunes into the stew and season to taste with salt and pepper. Using a dessertspoon, place spoonfuls of the dumpling mixture on the surface of the stew, spacing them slightly apart. Re-cover and cook gently for a further 15–20 minutes until the dumplings have risen and have a fluffy texture. Serve in shallow bowls.

mediterranean pork stew

what you need

Cost
££

Timing
🕐 🕐 🕐

Serves
2

- 1 tablespoon olive oil
- 250 g (8 oz) boneless lean pork, cut into chunks
- 1 red onion, cut into thin wedges
- 1 garlic clove, crushed
- 1 yellow pepper, cored, deseeded and chopped
- 8 artichoke hearts in oil, drained and quartered
- 200 g (7 oz) can chopped tomatoes
- 100 ml (3½ fl oz) red wine
- 50 g (2 oz) black olives, pitted
- grated zest of 1 lemon
- 1 bay leaf
- 1 sprig of thyme, plus extra to garnish
- garlic bread, to serve

what you do

1. Heat the oil in a flameproof casserole and fry the pork for 4–5 minutes until browned on all sides. Lift out with a slotted spoon on to a plate.
2. Add the onion, garlic and yellow pepper to the casserole and fry for 2 minutes. Return the pork to the casserole together with all the remaining ingredients.
3. Bring to the boil, then reduce the heat, cover and cook gently for 1 hour, or until the meat is tender. Garnish with sprigs of thyme and serve with garlic bread.

hoisin pork stir-fry

Cost
££

Timing

Serves
4

what you need

- 1 tablespoon hoisin sauce
- 1 tablespoon light soy sauce
- 1 tablespoon white wine vinegar
- 1 tablespoon vegetable oil
- 2 garlic cloves, sliced
- 1 teaspoon grated fresh root ginger
- 1 small red chilli, deseeded and sliced
- 250 g (8 oz) pork fillet, thinly sliced
- 175 g (6 oz) sugar snap peas
- 175 g (6 oz) broccoli florets
- 2 tablespoons water
- steamed rice, to serve

what you do

1. Combine the hoisin and soy sauces and vinegar in a mug and set aside.
2. Heat the oil in a wok until starting to smoke, add the garlic, ginger and chilli and stir-fry over a high heat for 10 seconds. Add the pork fillet and stir-fry for 2–3 minutes, or until golden. Lift out with a slotted spoon on to a plate.
3. Add the sugar snap peas and broccoli florets to the wok and stir-fry for 1 minute. Add the measured water and cook for a further 1 minute.
4. Return the pork to the wok, add the hoisin mixture and cook for 1 minute, or until the vegetables are cooked. Serve with steamed rice.

STUDENT TIP

Local farmers' markets overflow with great-value seasonal produce and this is the time to really put your freezer to work: wash and bag up seasonal berries; peel and chop apples and pears; and peel and dice vegetables — ready to prepare casseroles, compotes and soups.

sausage & onion traybake

what you need

Cost
£

Timing
◑ ◑

Serves
4

- 3 red onions, cut into wedges
- 3 red apples, cored and cut into 6 wedges
- 200 g (7 oz) baby carrots, scrubbed
- 3 potatoes, peeled and cut into small cubes

- 4 tablespoons olive oil
- 12 good-quality pork sausages
- 2 tablespoons chopped sage
- 1 tablespoon rosemary
- 3 tablespoons clear honey
- salt and pepper

what you do

1. Scatter the onions, apples, carrots and potatoes in a large roasting tin. Drizzle over the oil and toss well to lightly coat all the vegetables in the oil. Season generously with salt and pepper. Arrange the sausages in and around the vegetables, sprinkle over the herbs and toss again.

2. Bake in a preheated oven, 200°C (400°F), Gas Mark 6, for 20–22 minutes until golden and cooked through.

3. Remove from the oven and drizzle over the honey. Toss all the vegetables and sausages in the honey and serve.

chorizo & chickpea stew

Cost
£

Timing

Serves
4

what you need

- 1 teaspoon olive oil
- 2 red onions, chopped
- 2 red peppers, cored, deseeded and chopped
- 100 g (3½ oz) chorizo sausage, thinly sliced
- 500 g (1 lb) cooked new potatoes, sliced
- 500 g (1 lb) plum tomatoes, chopped, or 400 g (13 oz) can chopped tomatoes, drained
- 400 g (13 oz) can chickpeas, rinsed and drained
- 2 tablespoons chopped parsley, to garnish
- garlic bread, to serve

what you do

Heat the oil in a large frying pan and fry the onions and red peppers over a medium heat for 3–4 minutes. Add the chorizo and cook, turning frequently, for 2 minutes.

Stir the potatoes, tomatoes and chickpeas into the pan and bring to the boil. Reduce the heat and cook gently for 10 minutes. Garnish with the chopped parsley and serve with garlic bread to mop up all the juices.

sweet & sour pork

Cost
££

Timing
⏱ ⏱

Serves
4

- 1 tablespoon vegetable oil
- ½ pineapple, skinned, cored and cut into bite-sized chunks
- 1 onion, cut into chunks
- 1 orange pepper, cored, deseeded and cut into chunks
- 375 g (12 oz) pork fillet, cut into strips
- 100 g (3½ oz) mangetout, halved lengthways
- 6 tablespoons tomato ketchup
- 2 tablespoons soft light brown sugar
- 2 tablespoons white wine or malt vinegar
- cooked egg noodles, to serve (optional)

what you do

1. Heat the oil in a large wok and stir-fry the pineapple over a very high heat for 3–4 minutes until browned in places. Lift out with a slotted spoon on to a plate.
2. Add the onion and orange pepper to the wok and cook over a high heat, stirring frequently, for 5 minutes, or until softened. Add the pork and stir-fry for 5 minutes, or until browned and cooked through.
3. Return the pineapple to the wok together with the mangetout and cook, stirring occasionally, for 2 minutes.
4. Meanwhile, mix together the tomato ketchup, sugar and vinegar in a mug. Pour over the pork mixture, toss and cook for a further 1 minute to heat the sauce through. Serve immediately, with cooked egg noodles, if liked.

liver & onions

Cost
£

Timing
● ● ●

Serves
4

what you need

- 50 g (2 oz) butter
- 2 tablespoons olive oil
- 2 large onions, thinly sliced
- 625 g (1 ¼ 1b) calves' liver, thinly sliced (ask your butcher to slice as thinly as possible)
- 2 tablespoons finely chopped parsley, to garnish
- salt and pepper

what you do

1. Melt half the butter with the oil in a large heavy-based frying pan with a tight-fitting lid. Add the onions and season with salt and pepper, then cover, reduce the heat to its lowest setting and cook, stirring occasionally, for 35–40 minutes until very soft and golden. Lift out with a slotted spoon on to a plate.

2. Increase the heat to high and melt the remaining butter in the pan. Season the liver with salt and pepper. Once the butter starts foaming, add the liver and cook for 1–2 minutes until browned. Turn over the liver, return the onions to the pan and cook for a further 1 minute. Serve garnished with the chopped parsley.

STUDENT TIP

If it has a very long or non-existent use-by date then buy it in bulk. Look out for BOGOF (buy one, get one free) and half-price offers on things like toilet paper, pasta and other dried and canned goods.

bacon, pea & courgette risotto

what you need

Cost
£

Timing
⦿ ⦿

Serves
4

- 50 g (2 oz) butter
- 150 g (5 oz) streaky bacon, diced
- 300 g (10 oz) risotto rice
- 100 ml (3½ fl oz) dry white wine (optional)
- 900 ml (1½ pints) hot chicken or vegetable stock (see pages 109 or 34 for homemade) (add an extra 100 ml/3½ fl oz if not using wine)
- 2 courgettes, about 325 g (11 oz) in total, coarsely grated
- 200 g (7 oz) frozen peas, defrosted
- 1 small bunch of basil, shredded (optional)
- salt and pepper
- grated Parmesan cheese, to serve

what you do

1. Melt the butter in a large frying pan or saucepan and cook the bacon over a medium heat for 6–7 minutes until golden. Lift out half of the bacon with a slotted spoon on to a plate.

2. Add the rice to the pan and stir well. Pour in the wine, if using, and stock. Bring to the boil, then simmer gently for 15–18 minutes, stirring as often as possible, until the rice is tender and creamy. Stir in the courgette and peas for the final 2–3 minutes of the cooking time.

3. Season with salt and pepper, then spoon the risotto into 4 serving bowls. Scatter over the reserved bacon and the basil, if using. Serve sprinkled with grated Parmesan.

spicy sausage & tomato

Cost
£

Timing

Serves
4

what you need

- 2 tablespoons olive oil
- 8 thick, spicy Italian sausages, cut into 2 cm (¾ inch) pieces
- 1 red chilli, deseeded and finely chopped
- 4 garlic cloves, finely chopped
- 1 onion, finely chopped
- 1 teaspoon dried red chilli flakes
- 400 g (13 oz) can chopped tomatoes with herbs
- 1 teaspoon caster sugar
- 2 teaspoons chopped rosemary
- salt and pepper
- 4 tablespoons chopped parsley, to garnish

To serve
- cooked pasta, such as penne
- 100 g (3½ oz) Parmesan cheese, grated

what you do

1. Heat the oil in a large frying pan, add the sausages and fry over a high heat for 3–4 minutes until browned. Add the chilli, garlic, onion and chilli flakes and fry for a further 1–2 minutes.
2. Stir in the tomatoes, sugar and rosemary and bring to the boil, then reduce the heat to medium and cook for 8–10 minutes. Season with salt and pepper. Garnish with the chopped parsley, then serve with cooked pasta and grated Parmesan to sprinkle over.

beef & pickled onion stew

Cost	Timing	Serves
££	▶ ▶ ▶	4

- 3 tablespoons plain flour
- 1 kg (2 lb) braising steak, cut into large chunks
- 2 tablespoons olive oil
- 500 g (1 lb) jar pickled onions, drained
- 2 carrots, thickly sliced
- 300 ml (½ pint) beer
- 600 ml (1 pint) beef stock (see page 84 for homemade)
- 4 tablespoons tomato purée
- 1 tablespoon Worcestershire sauce
- 2 bay leaves
- salt and pepper
- chopped parsley, to garnish

what you do

1. Season the flour with salt and pepper on a plate. Coat the beef with the flour.
2. Heat the oil in a large flameproof casserole and fry the beef in batches until browned on all sides, lifting out with a slotted spoon on to a plate.
3. Return all the beef to the casserole. Stir in the pickled onions and carrots, then gradually blend in the beer and stock. Bring to the boil, stirring, then add the tomato purée, Worcestershire sauce and bay leaves and season with salt and pepper to taste.
4. Cover and cook in a preheated oven, 160°C (325°F), Gas Mark 3, for 2 hours, stirring halfway through, until the beef and vegetables are tender. Garnish with the chopped parsley and serve immediately.

beef & potato hash

 Cost
£

 Timing
◗ ◗ ◗

 Serves
4

what you need

- 2 tablespoons vegetable oil
- 750 g (1½ lb) minced beef
- 1 fennel bulb, trimmed and chopped
- 2 celery sticks, chopped
- 2 teaspoons cornflour
- 450 ml (¾ pint) beef stock (see page 84 for homemade)
- 3 tablespoons tomato purée
- 700 g (1 lb 7 oz) waxy potatoes, cut into 1.5 cm (¾ inch) chunks
- 4 star anise, broken into pieces and crushed using a pestle and mortar (or a rolling pin or empty wine bottle)
- 3 tablespoons soy sauce
- 1 tablespoon light muscovado sugar
- 15 g (½ oz) roughly chopped fresh coriander
- salt and pepper

what you do

1. Heat 1 tablespoon of the oil in a large heavy-based frying pan with a lid and fry the beef for 10 minutes, breaking up the mince with a wooden spoon and stirring until browned and all the moisture has evaporated. Push the meat to one side of the pan, add the remaining oil, fennel and celery and fry for 5 minutes, or until softened.
2. Blend the cornflour with a little of the stock in a mug, pour into the pan and stir to thicken. Add the remaining stock, tomato purée, potatoes and star anise and bring to a simmer, stirring. Reduce the heat, cover and cook gently for about 30 minutes until the potatoes are tender, stirring occasionally and adding a dash more water if the pan becomes dry.
3. Stir in the soy sauce and sugar and cook for a further 5 minutes, uncovered if necessary to thicken the juices. Season to taste with salt and pepper and stir in the coriander just before serving.

beef goulash

Cost
££

Timing
◑ ◑ ◑

Serves
8

what you need

- 4 tablespoons olive oil
- 1.5 kg (3 lb) braising steak, cut into large chunks
- 2 onions, sliced
- 2 red peppers, cored, deseeded and diced
- 1 tablespoon smoked paprika
- 2 tablespoons chopped marjoram
- 1 teaspoon caraway seeds
- 1 litre (1¾ pints) beef stock (see cooking tip for homemade)
- 5 tablespoons tomato purée
- salt and pepper
- French bread, to serve

what you do

1. Heat the oil in a flameproof casserole and fry the beef in batches until browned on all sides, lifting out with a slotted spoon on to a plate.
2. Add the onions and red peppers to the casserole and cook gently for 10 minutes, or until softened. Stir in the paprika, marjoram and caraway seeds and cook, stirring, for 1 minute.
3. Return the beef to the casserole. Add the stock and tomato purée, season to taste with salt and pepper and bring to the boil, stirring. Reduce the heat, cover and cook gently for 1¼-2 hours. If the sauce needs thickening, uncover for the final 30 minutes of the cooking time. Serve with French bread.

Cooking tip
For a homemade beef stock, place 750 g (1½ lb) shin of beef, cut into chunks, in a large saucepan and add 2 chopped onions, 2-3 chopped carrots, 2 roughly chopped celery sticks, 1 bay leaf, 1 bouquet garni, 4-6 black peppercorns and 1.8 litres (3 pints) cold water. Slowly bring to the boil, then reduce the heat, cover with a lid and simmer gently for 2 hours, skimming off any scum that rises to the surface. Strain through a fine sieve, discarding the solids, and leave to cool. Cover and store in the fridge for up to several days or freeze for up to 6 months. This makes about 1.5 litres (2½ pints).

west indian beef & bean stew

Cost £

Timing ◐ ◐

Serves 4

what you need

- 3 tablespoons sunflower oil
- 800 g (1 lb 10 oz) minced beef
- 6 cloves
- 1 onion, finely chopped
- 2 tablespoons medium curry powder
- 2 carrots, peeled and cut into 1 cm (½ inch) cubes
- 2 celery sticks, diced
- 1 tablespoon thyme
- 2 garlic cloves, crushed
- 4 tablespoons tomato purée
- 600 ml (1 pint) hot beef stock (see page 84 for homemade)
- 1 large potato, peeled and cut into 1 cm (½ inch) cubes
- 200 g (7 oz) canned black beans, rinsed and drained
- 200 g (7 oz) canned black-eyed beans, rinsed and drained
- salt and pepper
- lemon wedges, to serve

what you do

Heat the oil in a large heavy-based saucepan, add the beef and fry, stirring, over a medium-high heat for 5-6 minutes until browned.

Add the cloves, onion and curry powder and cook for 2-3 minutes until the onions are beginning to soften, then stir in the carrots, celery, thyme, garlic and tomato purée.

Pour in the beef stock to just cover the meat and stir well, then add the potato and beans and bring to the boil. Reduce the heat slightly and simmer for 20 minutes, uncovered, or until the potatoes and beef are tender, then season to taste with salt and pepper. Ladle the stew into serving bowls and serve with lemon wedges.

rustic lamb & potato curry

Cost £££   Timing ● ●   Serves 4

what you need

- 2 tablespoons vegetable oil
- 1 large onion, roughly chopped
- 625 g (1¼ lb) lean lamb, cut into cubes
- 1 small green chilli, roughly chopped (optional)
- 4 tablespoons korma curry paste
- 2 x 400 g (13 oz) cans chopped tomatoes
- 300 ml (½ pint) chicken stock (see page 109 for homemade)
- 2 unpeeled potatoes, roughly cut into cubes
- 50 g (2 oz) fresh coriander, roughly chopped
- 150 ml (¼ pint) natural yogurt

what you do

1. Heat the oil in a large heavy-based frying pan with a lid and cook the onion and lamb over a high heat, stirring frequently, for 5 minutes, or until the lamb is browned all over and the onion softened.
2. Add the chilli, if using, and cook, stirring, for 1 minute. Stir in the curry paste and cook, stirring, for a further 2 minutes. Add the tomatoes, stock and potatoes and bring to the boil. Reduce the heat, cover and simmer for 10 minutes, then remove the lid and cook for a further 10 minutes, or until the lamb is cooked through and the potatoes are tender.
3. Remove from the heat, then scatter over the coriander and spoon in the yogurt, ready to stir in and serve.

pollock & lentils

what you need

- 4 tablespoons olive oil
- 1 onion, finely chopped
- 4 garlic cloves, crushed
- 2 teaspoons finely chopped rosemary, savory or thyme
- 400 g (13 oz) can green lentils, rinsed and drained
- 400 g (13 oz) can chopped tomatoes
- 2 teaspoons caster sugar
- 150 ml (¼ pint) fish stock (see page 125 for homemade)
- 625 g (1¼ lb) skinless pollock fillets
- 4 tablespoons chopped parsley
- 50 g (2 oz) can anchovy fillets, drained and chopped
- salt and pepper
- garlic mayonnaise, to serve

what you do

1. Heat 2 tablespoons of the oil in a flameproof casserole and gently fry the onion for 6–8 minutes until lightly browned. Add the garlic and rosemary, savory or thyme and cook for about 2 minutes.

2. Stir the lentils into the casserole with the tomatoes, sugar and stock. Bring to a simmer, then cover and cook in a preheated oven, 180°C (350°F), Gas Mark 4, for 10 minutes. Check over the fish for any stray bones and cut into 8 pieces. Season with salt and pepper.

3. Stir the parsley and anchovies into the casserole. Nestle the fish down into the lentils and drizzle the fish with the remaining oil. Re-cover and return to the oven for a further 25 minutes, or until the fish is cooked through. Serve with spoonfuls of garlic mayonnaise.

mackerel & sesame noodles

what you need

- 2 large mackerel fillets, about 125 g (4 oz) each, cut into pieces
- 2 tablespoons teriyaki sauce
- 2 teaspoons sesame oil
- 1 tablespoon sesame seeds
- ½ bunch of spring onions, chopped
- 1 garlic clove, very thinly sliced
- 100 g (3½ oz) French beans, topped and tailed and diagonally sliced
- 400 ml (14 fl oz) fish stock (see page 125 for homemade)
- 150 g (5 oz) pack medium straight-to-wok rice noodles
- 1 teaspoon caster sugar
- teaspoon lime juice

what you do

1. Put the mackerel in a bowl with the teriyaki sauce and toss to coat the fish with the sauce.
2. Warm the oil in a saucepan, then add the sesame seeds, spring onions, garlic and beans and heat through gently for 2 minutes.
3. Pour in the stock and bring to a gentle simmer. Cover and cook for 5 minutes.
4. Stir the mackerel, noodles, sugar and lime juice into the pan and cook gently for 2 minutes, or until the mackerel is cooked and the broth is hot. Serve immediately.

smoked haddock cannelloni

 Cost ££

 Timing ◔ ◔

 Serves 4

what you need

- butter, for greasing
- 400 g (13 oz) skinless smoked haddock fillet, cut into pieces
- 300 ml (½ pint) boiling water
- 300 g (10 oz) watercress
- 200 ml (7 fl oz) crème fraîche
- 8 fresh lasagne sheets
- 50 g (2 oz) dried breadcrumbs
- salt and pepper

what you do

1. Lightly grease an ovenproof dish with butter. Place the haddock in a bowl, pour over the measured water and leave to stand for 3 minutes. Drain, reserving the water, and break up the fish.
2. Place the watercress in a sieve and pour over boiling water from the kettle until it has wilted. Lay the watercress on a sheet of kitchen paper and squeeze to get rid of excess water. Roughly chop the watercress, then mix it with the haddock and 2 tablespoons of the crème fraîche.
3. Divide the haddock mixture among the lasagne sheets, arranging it in a strip down the middle. Roll up the pasta and arrange snugly, seam-side down, in the prepared ovenproof dish.
4. Mix together the remaining crème fraîche with the haddock soaking water in a mug, season with salt and pepper and pour over the top of the pasta.
5. Scatter the breadcrumbs over the pasta, cover the dish with foil and bake in a preheated oven, 200°C (400°F), Gas Mark 6, for 20 minutes. Remove the foil and cook under a preheated hot grill until the breadcrumbs are golden.

paella

what You need

- 1 kg (2 lb) live mussels
- 4 garlic cloves
- 1 small bunch of mixed herbs
- 150 ml (¼ pint) dry white wine
- 2 litres (3½ pints) hot chicken stock (see page 109 for homemade) or water
- 4 tablespoons olive oil
- 4 small cleaned squid, cut into rings
- 1 large onion, finely chopped
- 1 red pepper, cored, deseeded and chopped
- 4 large ripe tomatoes, skinned (see page 23), deseeded and chopped
- 12 skinless, boneless chicken thighs, cut into bite-sized pieces
- 500 g (1 lb) paella rice
- large pinch of saffron threads, crumbled
- 125 g (4 oz) fresh or frozen peas
- 12 large raw peeled prawns
- salt and pepper

what You do

1. Scrub the mussels in cold water. Scrape off any barnacles and pull away the dark hairy beards. Discard any with damaged shells or open ones that do not close when tapped firmly with a knife. Set aside.
2. Slice 2 of the garlic cloves and crush the remainder. Place the sliced garlic in a large heavy-based saucepan with the herbs, wine and 150 ml (¼ pint) of the stock or water and season well with salt and pepper. Tip in the mussels, cover and cook, shaking the pan frequently, for 4–5 minutes until all the shells have opened. Lift out the mussels with a slotted spoon into a bowl, discarding any that remain closed. Strain the cooking liquid into a bowl and reserve.
3. Heat 2 tablespoons of the oil in the pan and fry the squid, stirring frequently, for 5 minutes. Add the onion, red pepper and crushed garlic and cook gently for 5 minutes, or until softened. Add the mussel cooking liquid and tomatoes and season with salt and pepper. Bring to the boil, then reduce the heat and cook gently, stirring, for 15–20 minutes until thickened. Transfer to a bowl.
4. Heat the remaining oil in the pan, add the chicken and fry for 5 minutes. Add the rice and cook, stirring, for 3 minutes.
5. Return the squid mixture to the pan, add one-third of the remaining stock and the saffron and bring to the boil, stirring. Cover and simmer, adding stock a little at a time, for 30 minutes, or until the chicken is cooked, the rice is tender and the liquid has been absorbed.
6. Taste and adjust the seasoning if needed. Add the peas and prawns and simmer, for 5 minutes, adding a little more stock if required. Return the mussels to the pan, cover and heat through for 5 minutes. Serve immediately.

baked cod with tomatoes & olives

what you need

- 250 g (8 oz) cherry tomatoes, halved
- 100 g (3½ oz) pitted black olives
- 2 tablespoons capers in brine, drained
- 4 sprigs of thyme, plus extra for garnish
- 4 cod fillets, about 175 g (6 oz) each
- 2 tablespoons extra virgin olive oil
- 2 tablespoons balsamic vinegar
- salt and pepper
- mixed leaf salad, to serve

what you do

1. Combine the tomatoes, olives, capers and thyme in a roasting tin. Nestle the cod fillets in the tin, drizzle over the oil and balsamic vinegar and season to taste with salt and pepper. Bake in a preheated oven, 200°C (400°F), Gas Mark 6, for 15 minutes.
2. Transfer the fish, tomatoes and olives to serving plates. Spoon the pan juices over the fish and serve immediately with a mixed leaf salad.

Variation

For steamed cod with lemon, arrange a cod fillet on each of 4 x 30 cm (12 inch) squares of foil. Top each with ½ teaspoon grated lemon zest, a squeeze of lemon juice, 1 tablespoon extra virgin olive oil and salt and pepper to taste. Seal the edges of the foil together to form parcels, transfer to a baking sheet and cook in a preheated oven, 200°C (400°F), Gas Mark 6, for 15 minutes. Remove from the oven and leave to rest for 5 minutes. Open the parcels and serve sprinkled with chopped parsley.

roast sea bass with potatoes & mushrooms

Cost
££

Timing
● ● ●

Serves
2

what you need

- 875 g (1¾ lb) potatoes, peeled and cut into 1 cm (½ inch) slices
- 2 garlic cloves, thinly sliced
- 3 tablespoons olive oil
- 250 g (8 oz) mixed wild mushrooms, sliced if large
- 4 sea bass fillets, about 175 g (6 oz) each
- ½ tablespoon chopped parsley
- salt and pepper
- extra virgin olive oil, for drizzling

what you do

1. Line a large roasting tin with greaseproof paper. Place the potato slices in the tin, stir in half the garlic and 2 tablespoons of the olive oil and season with salt and pepper. Spread the potatoes out in a single layer, then roast in a preheated oven, 240°C (475°F), Gas Mark 9, for 18–20 minutes until cooked through and golden. Remove from the oven and lift out the potatoes with a slotted spoon on to a plate.

2. Place the tin on the hob, add the remaining oil, the mushrooms and the remaining garlic and cook over a high heat, stirring frequently, until the mushrooms are tender. Season with salt and pepper and remove from the heat.

3. Return the roasted potatoes to the tin and stir well. Season the sea bass fillets with salt and pepper, then sit them, skin-side up, on top of the potatoes. Scatter with the parsley and drizzle the fish with the remaining olive oil. Return to the oven and roast for 10–12 minutes until the fish is cooked through. Serve immediately with a drizzle of extra virgin olive oil.

spicy prawn & pea pilau

- 1 tablespoon sunflower oil
- 1 tablespoon butter
- 1 large onion, finely chopped
- 2 garlic cloves, finely chopped
- 1 tablespoon medium or hot curry paste
- 250 g (8 oz) basmati rice
- 600 ml (1 pint) hot fish or vegetable stock (see pages 125 or 34 for homemade)
- 300 g (10 oz) frozen peas
- finely grated zest and juice of 1 large lime
- 20 g (¾ oz) fresh coriander, finely chopped
- 400 g (13 oz) ready-cooked peeled prawns
- salt and pepper

what you do

1. Heat the oil and butter in a heavy-based saucepan, add the onion and cook over a medium heat for 2–3 minutes until softened. Stir in the garlic and curry paste and cook for a further 1–2 minutes until fragrant, then add the rice and stir to coat well.

2. Stir in the stock, peas and lime zest, then season well with salt and pepper and bring to the boil. Cover tightly, then reduce the heat to low and cook for 12–15 minutes until the liquid is absorbed and the rice is tender.

3. Remove from the heat, then stir in the lime juice, coriander and prawns. Cover and leave to stand for a few minutes to allow the prawns to heat through before serving.

goats' cheese & pepper lasagne

what you need

Cost	Timing	Serves
££	⏱⏱⏱	4

- 325 g (11 oz) can or jar pimientos, drained and roughly chopped
- 6 tomatoes, skinned (see page 23) and roughly chopped
- 1 yellow pepper, cored, deseeded and finely chopped
- 2 courgettes, thinly sliced
- 75 g (3 oz) sun-dried tomatoes, thinly sliced
- 100 g (3½ oz) sun-dried tomato pesto
- 25 g (1 oz) basil

- 4 tablespoons olive oil
- 150 g (5 oz) soft goats' cheese, crumbled
- 600 ml (1 pint) ready-made cheese sauce
- 150 g (5 oz) dried egg lasagne
- 6 tablespoons grated Parmesan cheese
- salt and pepper
- mixed leaf salad, to serve

what you do

1. Place the pimientos in a bowl with the tomatoes, yellow pepper, courgettes, tomatoes and pesto. Tear the basil leaves and add to the bowl with the oil and a little salt and pepper. Mix together thoroughly.

2. Spoon a quarter of the tomato mixture into a 1.8 litre (3 pint) shallow ovenproof dish and dot with a quarter of the goats' cheese and 4 tablespoons of the cheese sauce. Cover with a third of the lasagne sheets in a layer, breaking them to fit where necessary. Repeat the layering, finishing with a layer of the tomato mixture and goats' cheese. Spoon over the remaining cheese sauce and sprinkle with the Parmesan. Bake in a preheated oven, 190°C (375°F), Gas Mark 5, for 50 minutes–1 hour until deep golden. Leave to stand for 10 minutes before serving with a mixed leaf salad.

veggie bean chilli

what you need

Cost £   Timing ◑ ◑   Serves 4

- 2 tablespoons vegetable oil
- 1 onion, finely chopped
- 1 red pepper, cored, deseeded and sliced
- 1 garlic clove, crushed
- 1 teaspoon ground cumin
- 1 teaspoon chipotle paste or a pinch of chilli powder
- 1 teaspoon dried oregano
- ½ teaspoon ground coriander
- 400 g (13 oz) can chopped tomatoes

- 400 g (13 oz) can black beans, rinsed and drained
- 150 g (5 oz) canned sweetcorn, drained
- salt and pepper

To serve
- soured cream
- handful of chopped fresh coriander
- grated Cheddar cheese
- tortilla chips

what you do

1. Heat the oil in a large flameproof casserole dish. Add the onion and cook for 5 minutes until softened, then add the red pepper, garlic, spices and herbs and cook for 30 seconds. Pour in the tomatoes and season to taste with salt and pepper. Bring to the boil, then reduce the heat and simmer for 10 minutes.

2. Add the beans and sweetcorn to the pan and cook for a further 3–4 minutes until heated through. Divide among serving bowls and top each portion with a spoonful of soured cream. Sprinkle with the chopped coriander and grated cheese and serve with tortilla chips.

middle eastern courgette, tomato & mint curry

Cost £

Timing ◐ ◐

Serves 4

- 2 tablespoons olive oil
- 2 onions, finely sliced
- 4 courgettes, cut into 1 cm (½ inch) cubes
- 2 x 400 g (13 oz) cans peeled plum tomatoes
- 2 garlic cloves, crushed
- 1 teaspoon mild chilli powder
- ¼ teaspoon ground turmeric
- 2 teaspoons dried mint
- salt and pepper
- small handful of finely chopped mint, to garnish

what you do

1. Heat the oil in a large heavy-based saucepan, add the onions and cook over a medium-low heat, stirring occasionally, for 6–8 minutes until softened. Add the courgettes and cook, stirring occasionally, for a further 5–6 minutes until tender.

2. Increase the heat to medium, add the tomatoes and garlic and cook for 10–12 minutes until the sauce is thickened. Stir in the chilli powder, turmeric and dried mint and cook for a further 2–3 minutes. Season well with salt and pepper. Ladle the curry into serving bowls and garnish with the mint.

spicy green bean, potato & pesto linguini

 Cost ££

 Timing

 Serves 4

what you need

- 200 g (7 oz) potatoes, peeled and cut into small cubes
- 200 g (7 oz) green beans, trimmed and halved
- 350 g (11½ oz) fresh linguine
- 2 red chillies, finely chopped
- 250 g (8 oz) shop-bought fresh green pesto
- salt and pepper
- grated pecorino cheese, to serve

what you do

1. Cook the potatoes in a large saucepan of lightly salted boiling water for 10–12 minutes until just tender, adding the beans and linguine 4 minutes before the end of the cooking time. Drain well, then return to the pan.
2. Mix together the chillies and pesto in a mug, then season well with salt and pepper. Spoon into the pasta mixture and toss to mix well. Divide among serving bowls and serve with grated pecorino cheese to sprinkle over.

green veg curry

Cost £ | **Timing** ●● | **Serves** 4

- 1 tablespoon sunflower oil
- 3 tablespoons Thai green curry paste (see page 113 for homemade)
- 2 red chillies, deseeded and finely sliced (optional)
- 400 ml (14 fl oz) can coconut milk
- 200 ml (7 fl oz) vegetable stock (see page 34 for homemade)
- 6 kaffir lime leaves or 1 tablespoon finely grated lime zest
- 2 tablespoons soy sauce
- 1 tablespoon soft brown sugar
- 200 g (7 oz) carrots, cut into thick batons
- 250 g (8 oz) butternut squash, peeled, deseeded and cut into 1.5 cm (¾ inch) cubes
- 100 g (3½ oz) sugar snap peas
- handful finely chopped fresh coriander
- juice of 1 lime
- steamed jasmine rice, to serve

what you do

1. Heat the oil in a large nonstick saucepan. Add the curry paste and chillies, if using, and stir-fry for 2–3 minutes.
2. Stir in the coconut milk, stock, lime leaves or lime zest, soy sauce, sugar, carrots and butternut squash. Simmer, uncovered for 6–8 minutes, stirring occasionally. Add the sugar snap peas and continue to simmer for 4–5 minutes.
3. Remove from the heat and stir in the coriander and lime juice. Ladle the curry into serving bowls and serve with steamed jasmine rice.

ranch-style eggs

what you need

- 2 tablespoons olive oil
- 1 onion, finely sliced
- 1 red chilli, deseeded and finely chopped
- 1 garlic clove, crushed
- 1 teaspoon ground cumin
- 1 teaspoon dried oregano
- 400 g (13 oz) canned cherry tomatoes
- 200 g (7 oz) roasted red and yellow peppers in oil (from a jar), drained and roughly chopped
- 4 eggs
- salt and pepper
- 4 tablespoons finely chopped fresh coriander, to garnish

what you do

1. Heat the oil in a large frying pan with a lid. Add the onion, chilli, garlic, cumin and oregano and fry gently for 5 minutes, or until softened.
2. Stir in the tomatoes and red and yellow peppers and cook for a further 5 minutes, adding a splash of water if the sauce looks dry. Season well with salt and pepper.
3. Make 4 hollows in the sauce and break an egg into each hollow. Cover and cook for 5 minutes, or until the eggs are just set. Serve immediately, garnished with the chopped coriander.

Variation

For a Mexican-style sauce, heat 2 tablespoons olive oil in a large frying pan and add 1 finely chopped onion, 1 finely chopped red chilli, 1 teaspoon each of ground cumin and dried oregano, 2 x 400 g (13 oz) cans cherry tomatoes and 200 g (7 oz) chopped roasted red peppers in oil (from a jar, drained). Season with salt and pepper, bring to the boil and cook over a medium heat for 12–15 minutes. Stir in a small handful of chopped coriander and serve over cooked pasta or rice.

pesto puff tart

Cost
££

Timing

Serves
4

what you need

- 375 g (12 oz) pack ready-rolled puff pastry
- 3 tablespoons shop-bought fresh green pesto
- 300 g (10 oz) yellow and red cherry tomatoes, halved
- 150 g (5 oz) mixed antipasti (artichokes, roasted peppers, mushrooms and aubergines), from a jar, drained
- 100 g (3½ oz) goats' cheese, crumbled
- basil leaves, to garnish

what you do

Lay the puff pastry on a baking sheet. Score a 2.5 cm (1 inch) margin around the edge and prick the base with a fork.

Top with the pesto, tomatoes, mixed antipasti and goats' cheese. Bake in a preheated oven, 200°C (400°F), Gas Mark 6, for 15–20 minutes. Garnish with the basil leaves and serve.

STUDENT TIP

Price comparison websites help you quickly locate the cheapest prices for your groceries. Forget about brand loyalty — follow the bargains to stretch your budget. Some supermarkets also now run a price-check on every shop and will apply the discount (if applicable) on your next visit.

Oh So Quick and Easy

buttery prawns
on toast

sticky lemon
chicken noodles

chicken breasts with mascarpone & tomatoes
sticky lemon chicken noodles
chicken drumstick jambalaya
chicken & spinach stew
chicken & beans
pork & tomato rice pot
thai green pork curry
pork & red pepper chilli
beef stew with garlic bread topping
creamy coconut beef rendang
pea & lamb korma
crispy fish pie
steamed lemon salmon & potatoes
baked cod parcels with beans & chorizo

smoked haddock kedgeree
oven-baked fish & chips with tomato salsa
mixed seafood casserole
buttery prawns on toast
mushroom stroganoff
tomato & chickpea stew
mustardy squash, carrot & sweet potato casserole
spiced black beans & cabbage
tarragon mushroom toasts
balsamic roast tomatoes
courgette & herb risotto
basic pizza dough
basic tomato sauce

chicken breasts with mascarpone & tomatoes

Cost £££ **Timing** **Serves** 4

what you do

1. Mix together the mascarpone and pesto in a bowl. Cut a horizontal slit in the side of each chicken breast to form a pocket. Fill the pockets with the mascarpone mixture.
2. Spread out the breadcrumbs on a plate. Season the chicken breasts with salt and pepper, rub them with 1 tablespoon of the oil and then roll them in the breadcrumbs until well coated.
3. Place the chicken breasts in a roasting tin, drizzle over another tablespoon of the oil and bake in a preheated oven, 200°C (400°F), Gas Mark 6, for 10 minutes.
4. Add the tomatoes to the tin, season with salt and pepper and drizzle with the remaining oil. Return to the oven for a further 5 minutes, or until the chicken is cooked through. Scatter over the pine nuts and serve with crusty bread, if liked.

what you need

- 4 tablespoons mascarpone cheese
- 4 teaspoons shop-bought fresh green pesto
- 4 skinless chicken breast fillets
- 100 g (3½ oz) dried breadcrumbs
- 3 tablespoons olive oil, plus extra for greasing
- 150 g (5 oz) cherry tomatoes
- 25 g (1 oz) toasted pine nuts
- salt and pepper
- crusty bread, to serve (optional)

sticky lemon chicken noodles

Cost ££ · **Timing** · **Serves** 4

- 2 tablespoons vegetable oil
- 300 g (10 oz) chicken fillets, cut into thin strips
- 200 g (7 oz) Tenderstem broccoli
- 2 garlic cloves, crushed
- 2 teaspoons finely grated fresh root ginger
- 1 red chilli, finely chopped
- finely grated zest and juice of 1 lemon
- 1 tablespoon clear honey
- 2 teaspoons light soy sauce
- 300 g (10 oz) ready-cooked egg noodles
- handful of roasted cashew nuts, to garnish

what you do

1. Heat a large wok until smoking hot. Add the oil and swirl around the pan, then add the chicken and cook for 1 minute. Add the broccoli and cook for a further 5 minutes, or until the chicken is nearly cooked through. Add the garlic, ginger and chilli to the wok and cook for 1 minute more. Then add the lemon zest and juice, honey and soy sauce and toss around the pan.
2. Add the noodles and a splash of water and cook until heated through. Divide among serving bowls, garnish with the cashew nuts and serve.

chicken drumstick jambalaya

Cost
££

Timing

Serves
4

what you need

- 1 tablespoon sunflower oil
- 8 skinless chicken drumsticks
- 1 onion, chopped
- 2 garlic cloves, crushed
- 2 celery sticks, sliced
- 1 red chilli, deseeded and chopped
- 1 green pepper, cored, deseeded and chopped
- 75 g (3 oz) chorizo sausage, sliced
- 250 g (8 oz) long-grain rice
- 500 ml (17 fl oz) chicken stock (see cooking tip for homemade)
- 1 bay leaf
- 3 tomatoes, cut into wedges
- dash of Tabasco sauce
- salt and pepper

what you do

1. Heat the oil in a large saucepan. Cut a few slashes across the thickest part of the drumsticks, add them to the pan and fry over a high heat for 5 minutes, turning occasionally. Add the onion, garlic, celery, chilli and green pepper and cook for a further 2-3 minutes until softened.
2. Add the chorizo, fry briefly, then add the rice, stirring to coat the grains in the pan juices. Pour in the stock, add the bay leaf and bring to the boil. Cover, reduce the heat and simmer for 20 minutes, stirring occasionally, until the stock has been absorbed and the rice is tender.
3. Stir in the tomatoes and Tabasco sauce and season to taste with salt and pepper. Heat through for 3 minutes before serving.

Cooking tip
For a homemade chicken stock, place 1 large chicken carcass or 500 g (1 lb) chicken bones in a large saucepan and add 2 halved, unpeeled onions, 2 roughly chopped carrots, 1 roughly chopped celery stick, several bay leaves and 1 teaspoon black or white peppercorns. Just cover with cold water and bring to a gentle simmer. Reduce the heat to its lowest setting and cook, uncovered, for 2 hours. Strain through a fine sieve and leave to cool. Cover and store in the fridge for up to several days or freeze for up to 6 months.

chicken & spinach stew

what you do

what you need

- 625 g (1¼ lb) skinless, boneless chicken thighs, thinly sliced
- 2 teaspoons ground cumin
- 1 teaspoon ground ginger
- 2 tablespoons olive oil
- 1 tablespoon tomato purée
- 2 x 400 g (13 oz) cans cherry tomatoes
- 50 g (2 oz) raisins
- 250 g (8 oz) ready-cooked Puy lentils
- 1 teaspoon grated lemon zest
- 150 g (5 oz) baby spinach leaves
- salt and pepper
- handful of chopped parsley, to garnish
- steamed couscous or rice, to serve

1. Mix the chicken with the cumin and ginger in a bowl until well coated. Heat the oil in a large saucepan, then add the chicken and cook for 2–3 minutes until lightly browned.
2. Stir in the tomato purée, tomatoes, raisins, lentils and lemon zest, season with salt and pepper and simmer gently for about 12 minutes until thickened slightly and the chicken is cooked.
3. Add the spinach and stir until wilted. Ladle the stew into bowls, then garnish with the chopped parsley and serve with steamed couscous or rice.

chicken & beans

what you do

1. Heat the oil in a heavy-based saucepan and cook the chicken and onion over a medium heat for 3–4 minutes.
2. Add the treacle, mustard, sugar and tomatoes, bring to the boil and then reduce the heat to simmer for 2 minutes. Stir in the beans and parsley and cook for a further 1 minute, or until heated through.
3. Spoon the mixture on to the slices of wholemeal toast, season with pepper and serve immediately.

what you need

- 1 tablespoon olive oil
- 2 boneless, skinless chicken breasts, each about 150 g (5 oz), thinly sliced
- 1 onion, thinly sliced
- 1 tablespoon black treacle
- 1 tablespoon wholegrain mustard
- 1 tablespoon soft dark brown sugar
- 400 g (13 oz) can chopped tomatoes
- 400 g (13 oz) can baked beans
- 3 tablespoons chopped parsley
- pepper
- 4 thick slices of wholemeal toast, to serve

pork & tomato rice pot

what you do

what you need

- 3 tablespoons olive oil
- 300 g (10 oz) pork fillet, sliced
- 1 onion, finely chopped
- 3 garlic cloves, finely chopped
- 250 g (8 oz) paella rice
- 2 teaspoons smoked paprika
- 200 g (7 oz) can chopped tomatoes
- 650 ml (1 pint 2 fl oz) hot chicken stock (see page 109 for homemade)
- 125 g (4 oz) baby spinach leaves
- salt and pepper
- lemon wedges, to serve

1. Heat 1 tablespoon of the oil in a large, deep frying pan with a lid. Add the pork fillet and cook over a high heat for 3 minutes, or until golden and nearly cooked through. Lift out with a slotted spoon on to a plate.
2. Reduce the heat, add the remaining oil and the onion to the pan and cook for 3 minutes, or until softened. Stir in the garlic and cook for 30 seconds, then stir in the rice and cook for 1 minute. Add the paprika and tomatoes, bring to the boil and then reduce the heat to simmer for 2–3 minutes.
3. Pour in the stock, season to taste with salt and pepper and cook for 12–15 minutes until there is just a little liquid left around the edges of the pan.
4. Lightly fork the spinach through the rice, arrange the pork on top, then cover and cook for a further 3–4 minutes until the pork is cooked through. Serve with lemon wedges.

thai green pork curry

Cost
£

Timing

Serves
1

- 2 tablespoons olive oil
- 4 boneless pork steaks, cut into bite-sized pieces
- 2 tablespoons Thai green curry paste (see cooking tip for homemade)
- 400 ml (14 fl oz) can coconut milk
- 100 g (3½ oz) green beans
- 200 g (7 oz) can water chestnuts, drained, rinsed and cut in half
- juice of 1 lime, or to taste
- 1 handful of fresh coriander leaves
- boiled rice, to serve

what you do

1. Heat the oil in a large saucepan, add the pork and cook, stirring, for 3–4 minutes until browned all over. Add the curry paste and cook, stirring, for 1 minute until fragrant.
2. Pour in the coconut milk, stir and reduce the heat to a gentle simmer. Cook for 10 minutes, then add the beans and water chestnuts and cook for a further 3 minutes.
3. Remove from the heat, add lime juice to taste and stir through the coriander. Serve immediately with boiled rice.

Cooking tip

For homemade Thai green curry paste, put 15 small green chillies, 4 halved garlic cloves, 2 finely chopped lemon grass stalks, 2 torn lime leaves, 2 chopped shallots, 50 g (2 oz) fresh coriander leaves, stalks and roots, 2.5 cm (1 inch) piece of fresh root ginger, peeled and finely chopped, 2 teaspoons black peppercorns, 1 teaspoon pared lime zest, ½ teaspoon salt and 1 tablespoon groundnut oil into a food processor or blender and process to a thick paste. Alternatively, use a pestle and mortar to crush the ingredients, working in the oil at the end. Transfer the paste to an airtight container; it can be stored in a fridge for up to 3 weeks.

pork & red pepper chilli

Cost £

Timing ⏱

Serves 4

what you need

- 2 tablespoons olive oil
- 1 large onion, chopped
- 2 garlic cloves, crushed
- 1 red pepper, cored, deseeded and diced
- 450 g (14½ oz) minced pork
- 1 red chilli, finely chopped
- 1 teaspoon dried oregano
- 500 g (1 lb) passata
- 400 g (13 oz) can red kidney beans, rinsed and drained
- salt and pepper

To serve
- soured cream
- fresh coriander, chopped
- boiled rice or crusty bread

what you do

1. Heat the oil in a saucepan, add the onion, garlic and red pepper and cook for 5 minutes, or until softened and starting to brown. Add the pork and cook, stirring and breaking up the mince with a wooden spoon, for 5 minutes, or until browned.
2. Add all the remaining ingredients to the pan and bring to the boil. Reduce the heat and simmer gently for 20 minutes. Remove from the heat and season well with salt and pepper. Divide among serving bowls, top with a dollop of soured cream and fresh coriander and serve with boiled rice or crusty bread.

Cooking tip
To serve this dish as a pasta salad, refresh the cooked pasta in cold running water before adding the remaining ingredients.

beef stew with garlic bread topping

Cost ££ **Timing** ⏱⏱ **Serves** 4

- 2 tablespoons olive oil
- 400 g (13 oz) beef steak, cut into chunks
- 1 onion, sliced
- 1 carrot, sliced
- 1 celery stick, sliced
- 1 teaspoon tomato purée
- 2 teaspoons plain flour
- handful of chopped thyme
- 100 ml (3½ fl oz) red wine
- 200 ml (7 fl oz) hot beef stock (see page 84 for homemade)
- ½ ready-made garlic bread baguette, sliced
- salt and pepper

what you do

1. Heat 1 tablespoon of the oil in a flameproof casserole over a high heat. Add the beef and cook for 2–3 minutes until golden. Lift out with a slotted spoon on to a plate.
2. Add the remaining oil to the casserole together with the onion, carrot and celery and cook for 5 minutes, or until softened. Stir in the tomato purée, flour and thyme, then pour in the wine and cook for 2–3 minutes until reduced by half. Pour in the stock and simmer for 15 minutes.
3. Return the meat to the casserole, season with salt and pepper and mix well. Arrange the garlic bread slices on top of the stew. Cook under a preheated hot grill for 3 minutes, or until the bread is golden and crisp.

creamy coconut beef rendang

Cost
££

Timing
🕐

Serves
4

what you need

- 2 tablespoons vegetable oil
- 1 tablespoon peeled and finely chopped fresh root ginger
- 1 bird's eye chilli, thinly sliced
- 1 garlic clove, thinly sliced
- 1 lemon grass stalk, thinly sliced
- 500 g (1 lb) frying steak, cut into strips
- ½ teaspoon ground cinnamon
- pinch of ground turmeric
- juice of 1 lime
- 400 g (13 oz) can coconut milk
- 4 tablespoons chopped fresh coriander
- steamed Thai jasmine rice, to serve (optional)

what you do

Heat the oil in a large, heavy-based frying pan or wok and cook the ginger, chilli, garlic and lemon grass over a medium heat, stirring frequently, for 1–2 minutes until softened but not coloured. Add the beef, increase the heat to high and stir-fry for 5 minutes, or until browned and cooked through.

Stir in the cinnamon and turmeric and cook, stirring, for a few seconds before adding the lime juice and coconut milk. Gently heat, stirring, for 2–3 minutes until the sauce is hot. Serve immediately with the steamed jasmine rice, if liked, and scatter with the chopped coriander.

pea & lamb korma

Cost **££**

Timing

Serves **4**

- 2 tablespoons olive oil
- 1 onion, chopped
- 2 garlic cloves, crushed
- 250 g (8 oz) potatoes, cut into 1.5 cm (¾ inch) dice
- 500 g (1 lb) minced lamb
- 1 tablespoon korma curry powder
- 200 g (7 oz) frozen peas
- 200 ml (7 fl oz) vegetable stock (see page 34 for homemade)
- 2 tablespoons mango chutney
- salt and pepper
- chopped fresh coriander, to garnish

To serve
- natural yogurt
- fresh chilli
- steamed rice

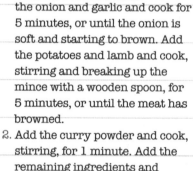

what you do

1. Heat the oil in a saucepan, add the onion and garlic and cook for 5 minutes, or until the onion is soft and starting to brown. Add the potatoes and lamb and cook, stirring and breaking up the mince with a wooden spoon, for 5 minutes, or until the meat has browned.

2. Add the curry powder and cook, stirring, for 1 minute. Add the remaining ingredients and season to taste with salt and pepper. Bring to the boil, then reduce the heat, cover tightly and simmer for 20 minutes. Divide among serving bowls, garnish with the chopped coriander and serve with natural yogurt, one fresh chilli and steamed rice.

crispy fish pie

Cost
£££

Timing

Serves
4

what you need

- butter, for greasing
- 200 g (7 oz) frozen spinach
- 400 g (13 oz) skinless salmon fillet, cubed
- 250 g (8 oz) skinless smoked haddock fillet, cubed
- 4 eggs
- 100 ml (3½ fl oz) crème fraîche
- 2 tablespoons boiling water
- 50 g (2 oz) dried breadcrumbs
- salt and pepper

what you do

1. Lightly grease an ovenproof dish with butter. Place the spinach in a sieve and pour over boiling water from the kettle until it has defrosted. Lay the spinach on a sheet of kitchen paper and squeeze to get rid of excess water.
2. Arrange the spinach in the prepared ovenproof dish and place the fish on top. Make 4 small hollows between the fish pieces and crack an egg into each one.
3. Mix the crème fraîche with the measured water in a mug, season to taste with salt and pepper and pour over the fish.
4. Sprinkle the breadcrumbs over the top of the pie. Place in a preheated oven, 200°C (400°F), Gas Mark 6, for 25 minutes, or until golden and bubbling and the fish is cooked through.

steamed lemon salmon & potatoes

Cost
££

Timing

Serves
2

what you need

- 400 g (13 oz) new potatoes, sliced
- 2 salmon fillets
- 75 g (3 oz) French beans, topped and tailed
- 4 tablespoons crème fraîche
- finely grated zest and juice of ½ lemon
- handful of chopped dill
- 1 tablespoon capers, rinsed and drained
- salt and pepper

what you do

1. Set a large steamer over a saucepan of gently simmering water. Place the potatoes in the steamer and season well with salt and pepper. Cover and cook for 10 minutes.

2. Place the salmon on top of the potatoes and scatter around the beans. Cover and cook for a further 7–10 minutes until the fish and vegetables are cooked through.

3. Meanwhile, mix together the crème fraîche, lemon zest and juice, dill and capers in a mug and season to taste with salt and pepper. Serve the salmon and vegetables with the crème fraîche mixture.

STUDENT TIP

Student kitchens are a favourite hangout for germs and dirty cloths are germ magnets. If you're unsure of when the dishcloths last had a wash, rinse and squeeze them, then lay out flat in the microwave and zap them for 2-3 minutes.

baked cod parcels with beans & chorizo

what you do

1. Cut 4 large sheets of baking paper and place a cod fillet on each. Divide the beans, tomatoes and thyme among the cod fillets.

2. Place a chorizo slice on top of each piece of fish and season well with salt and pepper, then fold the paper over and roll up the edges to create airtight parcels, leaving just a little gap.

3. Pour a little wine into each parcel and then fully seal, leaving enough space in the packages for air to circulate. Place on a baking sheet and bake in a preheated oven, 220°C (425°F), Gas Mark 7, for 15 minutes, or until the fish is cooked through.

what you need

- 4 cod fillets
- 400 g (13 oz) can butter beans, rinsed and drained
- 125 g (4 oz) cherry tomatoes, halved
- 4 sprigs of thyme
- 4 thin slices of chorizo sausage
- 75 ml (3 fl oz) dry white wine
- salt and pepper

smoked haddock kedgeree

Cost ££

Timing ◐ ◐

Serves 4

what you do

1. Heat the oil and butter in a large saucepan. Add the onion and cook for 5 minutes, then stir in the garlic and ginger and cook for 1 minute. Add the cumin and coriander seeds and cook for 30 seconds, then stir in the curry powder, turmeric and rice and cook for a further 1 minute.

2. Pour in the stock and cook for 5 minutes. Place the fish on top of the rice and cook for a further 5 minutes. By this time, most of the stock should have boiled away.

3. Add the peas, cover the pan tightly with a lid, turn down the heat as low as it will go and cook for 5–7 minutes until the rice is cooked through.

4. Use a fork to gently break up the fish, stir the fish and peas into the rice and season to taste with salt and pepper. Scatter with the chilli and coriander and serve with mango chutney.

what you need

- 1 tablespoon vegetable oil
- 25 g (1 oz) butter
- 1 onion, finely chopped
- 1 garlic clove, crushed
- 1 teaspoon finely grated fresh root ginger
- 1 teaspoon cumin seeds
- ½ teaspoon coriander seeds
- 1 teaspoon curry powder
- ½ teaspoon ground turmeric
- 300 g (10 oz) basmati rice
- 650 ml (1 pint 2 fl oz) hot chicken or fish stock (see pages 109 or 125 for homemade)
- 300 g (10 oz) skinless smoked haddock fillet
- 75 g (3 oz) frozen peas
- 1 red chilli, chopped
- handful of chopped fresh coriander
- salt and pepper
- mango chutney, to serve

oven-baked fish & chips with tomato salsa

Cost
££

Timing

Serves
4

what you need

- 750 g (1½ lb) potatoes, cut into thin wedges
- 4 tablespoons olive oil
- 4 skinless cod or haddock fillets
- finely grated zest of 1 lemon
- 1 teaspoon balsamic vinegar
- 4 tomatoes, chopped
- 1 teaspoon capers, rinsed and drained
- 1 spring onion, chopped
- salt and pepper
- handful of chopped parsley, to garnish

what you do

1. Place the potatoes in a roasting tin. Drizzle over half the oil, season well with salt and pepper and toss to make sure the potatoes are coated in oil. Bake in a preheated oven, 220°C (425°F), Gas Mark 7, for 10 minutes.

2. Turn over the potatoes, place the fish on top, season again and scatter over the lemon zest. Return to the oven for a further 15–20 minutes until the potatoes are just cooked through.

3. Meanwhile, make the tomato salsa. Mix together the remaining oil and the vinegar in a bowl and season to taste with salt and pepper. Stir in the tomatoes, capers and spring onion.

4. Transfer the fish to serving plates, garnish with the chopped parsley and serve with the chips and salsa on the side.

mixed seafood casserole

Cost
££

Timing
🕐

Serves
4

what you need

- 4 tablespoons olive oil
- 1 onion, diced
- 4 garlic cloves, crushed
- 100 ml (3½ fl oz) white wine
- 400 g (13 oz) can chopped tomatoes
- 200 ml (7 fl oz) fish stock (see cooking tip for homemade)
- pinch of saffron threads
- 400 g (13 oz) pack ready-cooked mixed seafood
- 2 tablespoons chopped parsley
- crusty bread, to serve (optional)

1. Heat the oil in a heavy-based saucepan and sauté the onion and garlic for 3–4 minutes. Pour in the wine and boil for 2–3 minutes, then add the tomatoes, stock and saffron. Bring to a simmer, stir in the mixed seafood and parsley and cook for 5–6 minutes to heat through. Serve with crusty bread, if liked.

Cooking tip
For homemade fish stock, melt 15 g (½ oz) butter in a large saucepan and gently fry 1 kg (2 lb) white fish bones and trimmings until the trimmings have turned opaque. Add a quartered onion, 2 roughly chopped celery sticks, a handful of parsley, several lemon slices and 1 teaspoon peppercorns. Cover with cold water and bring to a gentle simmer. Cook very gently for 30–35 minutes. Strain through a sieve and leave to cool. Cover and chill for up to 2 days or freeze for up to 3 months.

buttery prawns on toast

- 100 g (3½ oz) butter
- pinch of cayenne pepper
- 300 g (10 oz) raw prawns, peeled
- 1 tablespoon lemon juice
- 2 tablespoons chopped chives
- salt and pepper
- 4 slices of granary toast, to serve

what you do

1. Place a large frying pan over a medium heat and melt the butter with the cayenne pepper. Once the butter begins to froth slightly, add the prawns and cook for 2-3 minutes, stirring occasionally, until they are pink and cooked through.
2. Add the lemon juice, then stir in the chives and season to taste with salt and pepper. Spoon the prawns and their buttery juices on to the granary toast and serve immediately.

mushroom stroganoff

what you need

- 1 tablespoon butter
- 2 tablespoons olive oil
- 1 onion, thinly sliced
- 4 garlic cloves, finely chopped
- 500 g (1 lb) chestnut mushrooms, sliced
- 2 tablespoons wholegrain mustard
- 250 ml (8 fl oz) crème fraîche
- salt and pepper
- 3 tablespoons chopped parsley, to garnish

Cost £   Timing   Serves 4

what you do

1. Melt the butter with the oil in a large frying pan, add the onion and garlic and cook until softened and starting to brown.
2. Add the mushrooms to the pan and cook until softened and starting to brown. Stir in the mustard and crème fraîche and just heat through. Season to taste with salt and pepper, then serve immediately, garnished with the chopped parsley.

tomato & chickpea stew

Cost £	Timing ⏱⏱	Serves 4

what you need

- 2½ tablespoons olive oil
- 1 large onion, chopped
- 1 green pepper, cored, deseeded and chopped
- 1 garlic clove, chopped
- 2.5 cm (1 inch) piece of fresh root ginger, peeled and chopped
- 1 teaspoon ground cumin
- 1 teaspoon ground coriander
- 2 tablespoons tomato purée
- 500 ml (17 fl oz) hot vegetable stock (see page 34 for homemade)
- 4 large tomatoes, each cut into 8 wedges
- 2 x 400 g (13 oz) cans chickpeas, rinsed and drained
- salt and pepper
- 2 tablespoons chopped parsley, to garnish

what you do

1. Heat the oil in a large heavy-based saucepan. Add the onion, green pepper, garlic and ginger, and cook for 6–7 minutes until softened.
2. Stir in the cumin and coriander and cook for a further 1 minute. Add the tomato purée, stock, tomatoes and chickpeas, then cover and bring to the boil. Season generously with salt and pepper, reduce the heat and simmer for 8 minutes, or until thickened slightly and the tomatoes have softened. Ladle the stew into serving bowls and serve garnished with the chopped parsley.

mustardy squash, carrot & sweet potato casserole

Cost £

Timing 🕐 🕐

Serves 4

what you do

1. Heat the oil in a heavy-based saucepan. Cook the onion and garlic for 3–4 minutes, until softened. Add the squash, sweet potatoes and carrots and cook for a further 3–4 minutes until lightly golden.
2. Pour in the wine, add the tarragon or rosemary and cook until reduced by half. Add the stock and mustard to the pan, then season generously with salt and pepper, bring to the boil and then reduce the heat to simmer gently for 15 minutes, or until the vegetables are tender.
3. Tip the spinach into the pan and stir until wilted. Serve with steamed couscous or rice.

what you need

- 3 tablespoons vegetable oil
- 1 red onion, roughly chopped
- 4 garlic cloves, chopped
- 750 g (1½ lb) butternut squash, peeled, deseeded and cut into bite-sized chunks
- 500 g (1 lb) sweet potatoes, peeled and cut into bite-sized chunks
- 2 carrots, cut into bite-sized chunks
- 125 ml (4 fl oz) dry white wine
- 1 teaspoon dried tarragon or rosemary
- 400 ml (14 fl oz) hot vegetable stock (see page 34 for homemade)
- 2 tablespoons wholegrain mustard
- 200 g (7 oz) spinach, washed, drained and shredded
- salt and pepper
- steamed couscous or rice, to serve

spiced black beans & cabbage

what you need

- 40 g (1½ oz) butter
- 1 large onion, chopped
- 150 g (5 oz) baby carrots, scrubbed
- 1 tablespoon ras el hanout spice blend
- 500 ml (17 fl oz) vegetable stock (see page 34 for homemade)
- 200 g (7 oz) new potatoes, scrubbed and diced
- 400 g (13 oz) can black beans, rinsed and drained
- 175 g (6 oz) cabbage
- salt (optional)

what you do

1. Melt the butter in a saucepan and gently fry the onion and carrots for 5 minutes, or until the onion is softened. Add the spice blend and fry for a further 1 minute.
2. Pour in the stock and bring to the boil. Reduce the heat to its lowest setting and stir in the potatoes and beans. Cover and cook gently for 15 minutes, or until the vegetables are tender and the juices slightly thickened.
3. Cut away the thick stalks from the cabbage and discard, then roll up the leaves and finely shred. Add to the pan and cook for a further 5 minutes. Season with salt, if necessary, and serve.

tarragon mushroom toasts

Cost £

Timing ◑ ◑

Serves 4

what you do

1. Toast the brioche slices lightly and keep warm.
2. Heat the butter in a frying pan and sauté the shallots, garlic and chilli, if using, for 1–2 minutes. Add the mushrooms and stir-fry over a medium heat for 6–8 minutes. Season well with salt and pepper, then remove from the heat and stir in the crème fraîche and herbs.
3. Spoon the mushrooms on to the toasted brioche and serve immediately, with an extra dollop of crème fraîche, if liked.

what you need

- 8 slices of brioche
- 150 g (5 oz) butter
- 2 banana shallots, finely chopped
- 3 garlic cloves, finely chopped
- 1 red chilli, deseeded and finely chopped (optional)
- 300 g (10 oz) mixed wild mushrooms, such as chanterelle, cep, girolle and oyster, or white mushrooms, trimmed and sliced
- 4 tablespoons crème fraîche, plus extra to garnish (optional)
- 2 tablespoons finely chopped tarragon
- 1 tablespoon finely chopped parsley
- salt and pepper

balsamic
roast tomatoes

Cost
££

Timing

Serves
4

what you need

- 12 plum tomatoes, about 700 g (1 lb 7 oz)
- 2 tablespoons olive oil
- 2 teaspoons balsamic vinegar
- 1 small bunch of basil, leaves torn
- 2 tablespoons pine nuts
- 1 small ciabatta
- salt and pepper

what you do

1. Halve the tomatoes and arrange, cut-side uppermost, in a roasting tin. Drizzle with the oil and vinegar. Tear half the basil leaves over the top, add the pine nuts and season with salt and pepper. Roast in a preheated oven, 180°C (350°F), Gas Mark 4, for 35–40 minutes until tender.
2. Cut the ciabatta in half lengthways then half again to give 4 quarters. Toast the cut side of the bread only, then transfer to serving plates and spoon the tomatoes on top. Tear the remaining basil leaves over the top and serve immediately.

STUDENT TIP

Sign up for loyalty cards at all the big supermarkets and collect points for your shopping. You can choose to use these on your grocery bill or swap them for vouchers or other deals. The value of points varies between retailers so check who's currently offering the best value.

courgette & herb risotto

Cost	Timing	Serves
££	● ●	4

- 4 tablespoons butter
- 2 tablespoons olive oil
- 1 large onion, finely chopped
- 2 garlic cloves, finely chopped
- 350 g (11½ oz) risotto rice
- 200 ml (7 fl oz) white wine
- 1.5 litres (2½ pints) vegetable stock, heated to simmering (see page 34 for homemade)
- 200 g (7 oz) baby spinach leaves, chopped
- 100 g (3½ oz) courgettes, finely diced
- 50 g (2 oz) Parmesan cheese, finely grated
- 1 small handful of dill, mint and chives, roughly chopped
- salt and pepper

what you do

1. Melt the butter with the oil in a saucepan, add the onion and garlic and cook for about 3 minutes until softened. Add the rice and stir until coated with the butter mixture. Pour in the wine and cook rapidly, stirring, until it has evaporated.

2. Add the stock, a ladleful at a time, and cook, stirring constantly, until each addition has been absorbed before adding the next. Continue until all the stock has been absorbed and the rice is creamy and cooked but still retains a little bite – this will take around 15 minutes.

3. Stir in the spinach and courgettes and heat through for 3–5 minutes. Remove from the heat and stir in the Parmesan and herbs. Season to taste with salt and pepper and serve immediately.

basic pizza dough

what you need

- 7 g (¼ oz) fresh yeast or 1 teaspoon dried yeast
- pinch of caster sugar
- 500 g (1 lb) plain flour, plus extra for dusting
- 350 ml (12 fl oz) lukewarm water
- 1½ teaspoons salt
- olive oil, for oiling

what you do

1. Dissolve the yeast in a bowl with the sugar, 2 tablespoons of the flour and 50 ml (2 fl oz) of the measured water. Leave to stand for 5 minutes until it starts to form bubbles.
2. Add the remaining water, the salt and half the remaining flour and stir with one hand until you have a paste-like mixture. Gradually add all the remaining flour, working the mixture until you have a moist dough. Shape the dough into a ball, cover with a moist tea towel and leave to rest in a warm place for 5 minutes.
3. Lightly dust a work surface with flour and knead the dough for 10 minutes, or until smooth and elastic. Shape into 4 equal-sized balls and place, spaced apart, on a lightly oiled baking sheet. Cover with a moist tea towel and leave to rise in a warm place for 1 hour. Use according to your recipe.

basic tomato sauce

what you need

- 2 teaspoons olive oil
- 1 garlic clove, finely chopped
- 1 kg (2 lb) canned chopped tomatoes
- large pinch of caster sugar
- 5 basil leaves (optional)
- salt

what you do

1. Heat the oil in a heavy-based saucepan over a medium heat. Add the garlic and cook for 30 seconds, stirring, then add the tomatoes, sugar and basil, if using. Season lightly with salt and bring to the boil.
2. You now have two options. If you want a very light sauce to spoon over stuffed fresh pasta or if your sauce will be used in another recipe where it will undergo further cooking, simmer the sauce over a medium heat for 2-3 minutes. Alternatively, if you are aiming for a more robust, concentrated tomato sauce to stir into pasta, simmer the sauce over a low heat for 40-45 minutes until thick and rich. The sauce can be eaten chunky or blended with a hand-held blender until smooth, then reheated.

Slowly Does It

balsamic braised
pork chops

monday sausage stew

turkey &
ham casserole

baked seafood
with paprika

chicken & sweet potato wedges ....

balsamic braised pork chops ....

easy lamb & barley risotto ....

monday sausage stew ....

jerk pork with pineapple salsa ....

baked seafood with paprika ....

turkey & ham casserole ....

chicken & sweet potato wedges

Cost
£

Timing
⏱ ⏱ ⏱

Serves
4

what you need

- 4 sweet potatoes, about 1.25 kg (2½ lb) in total, scrubbed and cut into thick wedges
- 4 boneless, skinless chicken thighs, cut into chunks
- 1 red onion, cut into wedges
- 4 plum tomatoes, cut into chunks
- 150 g (5 oz) chorizo sausage, skinned and sliced or diced, if very large
- leaves from 3 sprigs of rosemary
- 4 tablespoons olive oil
- salt and pepper
- watercress salad, to serve (optional)

what you do

1. Put the sweet potatoes in a large roasting tin with the chicken, onion and tomatoes. Tuck the chorizo in and around the sweet potatoes, then sprinkle with the rosemary and some salt and pepper. Drizzle with the oil.

2. Roast in a preheated oven, 200°C (400°F), Gas Mark 6, for about 35 minutes, turning once or twice, until the chicken is golden and cooked through and the sweet potato wedges are browned and tender. Spoon on to serving plates and serve with a watercress salad, if liked.

VARIATION

For mixed roots with fennel and chicken, use a mixture of 1.25 kg (2½ lb) baking potatoes, parsnips and carrots. Scrub the potatoes and peel the parsnips and carrots, then cut the root vegetables into wedges. Add to the roasting tin with the chicken as above. Sprinkle with 2 teaspoons fennel seeds, 1 teaspoon ground turmeric and 1 teaspoon paprika, then drizzle with 4 tablespoons olive oil and roast as above.

balsamic braised pork chops

what you need

Cost ££ **Timing** ⏱⏱⏱ **Serves** 4

- 4 spare rib pork chops, about 750 g (1½ lb) in total
- 3 tablespoons balsamic vinegar
- 2 tablespoons light muscovado sugar
- 2 onions, thinly sliced
- 2 dessert apples, peeled, cored and quartered
- 2 tablespoons cornflour
- 3 teaspoons English mustard
- 200 ml (7 fl oz) boiling chicken stock (see page 109 for homemade)
- chopped chives, to garnish (optional)

To serve
- mashed potato
- Brussel sprouts

what you do

1. Preheat the slow cooker if necessary; see the manufacturer's instructions. Arrange the pork chops in the base of the slow cooker pot and spoon over the vinegar and sugar. Sprinkle the onions on top, then add the apples.
2. Put the cornflour and mustard in a mug and blend with a little cold water to make a smooth paste, then gradually stir in the stock until smooth and pour over the pork. Cover with the lid and cook on high for 30 minutes. Reduce the heat and cook on low for 6½–7½ hours until the pork is cooked through and tender.
3. Transfer the pork to serving plates, stir the sauce and spoon over the chops. Sprinkle with chopped chives, if liked. Serve with mashed potatoes and steamed Brussels sprouts.

easy lamb & barley risotto

Cost
£££

Timing
▶ ▶ ▶

Serves
4

what you need

- 20 g (¾ oz) mixed dried mushrooms
- 1 litre (1¾ pints) boiling vegetable stock (see page 34 for homemade)
- 4 tablespoons cream sherry or fresh orange juice
- 1 onion, finely chopped
- 1 teaspoon ground cumin
- 2 garlic cloves, finely chopped
- 40 g (1½ oz) sultanas
- 125 g (4 oz) pearl barley
- 4 lamb chump chops, about 150 g (5 oz) each
- 250 g (8 oz) pumpkin or butternut squash, peeled, deseeded and cut into 2 cm (¾ inch) dice
- salt and pepper
- chopped mint and parsley, to garnish
- harissa, to serve

what you do

1. Preheat the slow cooker if necessary; see the manufacturer's instructions. Put the dried mushrooms in the slow cooker pot, pour in the stock, then stir in the sherry or orange juice, onion, cumin, garlic, sultanas and barley and season with salt and pepper. Arrange the chops on top in a single layer, season with salt and pepper, then tuck the pumpkin or squash into the gaps between the chops. Press the chops and pumpkin or squash down lightly into the stock, then cover with the lid and cook on low for 7–8 hours until the lamb and vegetables are tender.

2. Lift the chops out of the slow cooker and break them into pieces. Stir the risotto well, then spoon on to serving plates, top with the chops and garnish with the chopped herbs. Serve with spoonfuls of harissa, if liked.

monday sausage stew

Cost
£

Timing
▶ ▶ ▶

Serves
4

what you need

500 g (1 lb) pork chipolatas
1 onion, chopped
2 x 415 g (13½ oz) cans baked beans
2 tablespoons Worcestershire sauce
1 teaspoon dried mixed herbs
1 teaspoon Dijon mustard
200 ml (7 fl oz) boiling chicken stock (see page 109 for homemade)
300 g (10 oz) pumpkin or butternut squash, peeled, deseeded and cut into 2 cm (¾ inch) cubes
salt and pepper
garlic bread, to serve (optional)

what you do

1. Preheat the slow cooker if necessary; see the manufacturer's instructions. Grill the sausages on one side only.
2. Put the onion, baked beans and Worcestershire sauce in the slow cooker pot. Stir in the herbs, mustard and stock, then mix in the pumpkin or squash. Season with salt and pepper. Arrange the sausages on top, browned-sides uppermost, and press them into the liquid. Cover with the lid and cook on low for 7–8 hours until the sausages are cooked through and the pumpkin or squash is tender. Spoon into shallow serving bowls and serve with garlic bread, if liked.

STUDENT TIP

It might sound obvious, but don't wait until you're ready to cook to check you have all the ingredients needed for a recipe. Go through the cupboards in the morning so you can pick up any missing items while you're out and about.

jerk pork with pineapple salsa

Cost
££

Timing

Serves
4

what You need

- 750–875 g (1½–1¾ lb) pork shoulder joint
- 2 tablespoons powdered jerk spice mix
- 4 teaspoons light muscovado sugar
- 1 onion, roughly chopped
- 1 carrot, sliced
- 200 ml (7 fl oz) boiling chicken stock (see page 109 for homemade)
- salt and pepper
- boiled rice, to serve (optional)

Pineapple salsa
- 1 small pineapple, skinned, cored and finely chopped
- 2 teaspoons light muscovado sugar
- 1 large red chilli, halved, deseeded and finely chopped
- grated zest of 1 lime

what You do

1. Preheat the slow cooker if necessary; see the manufacturer's instructions. Remove the string from the pork, then cut away the skin. Unroll and, if needed, make a slit in the meat so that it can be opened out to make a strip that is of an even thickness. Rub the pork all over with the jerk spice mix, sugar and salt and pepper. Put the pork in the slow cooker pot, then scatter the onion and carrot into the gaps around the pork. Pour in the stock, cover with the lid and cook on high for 5–6 hours until the meat is very tender and almost falls apart.
2. Meanwhile, put the pineapple in a bowl with the sugar, chilli and lime zest. Mix together, then cover with clingfilm and chill until the pork is ready.
3. Lift the pork out of the slow cooker pot, remove any fat, then shred the meat with 2 forks. Serve with the salsa and boiled rice, if liked.

baked seafood with paprika

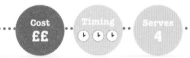

Cost ££   **Timing** ▸ ▸ ▸   **Serves** 4

what you need

- 1 onion, finely chopped
- 1 red pepper, cored, deseeded and diced
- 2 garlic cloves, finely chopped
- 400 g (13 oz) can chopped tomatoes
- 150 ml (¼ pint) dry white wine or fish stock (see page 125 for homemade)
- large pinch of paprika
- 2 sprigs of thyme
- 1 tablespoon olive oil
- 400 g (13 oz) pack frozen seafood (prawns, mussels, squid), defrosted
- salt and pepper
- chopped parsley, to garnish
- cooked pasta, such as tagliatelle, to serve

what you do

1. Preheat the slow cooker if necessary; see the manufacturer's instructions. Put the onion, red pepper, garlic and tomatoes into the slow cooker pot, then add the wine or stock, paprika, thyme, oil and a little salt and pepper. Cover with the lid and cook on low for 5–7 hours.
2. Rinse the seafood with cold water, drain and then stir into the slow cooker pot. Re-cover and cook on high for 30 minutes, or until piping hot. Garnish with the chopped parsley and serve with cooked pasta.

turkey & ham casserole

Cost
££

Timing

Serves
6

what you need

- 2 tablespoons plain flour
- 625 g (1¼ lb) turkey breast meat
- 50 g (2 oz) butter
- 2 onions, chopped
- 2 celery sticks, sliced
- 750 ml (1¼ pints) chicken stock (see page 109 for homemade)
- 1 tablespoon chopped thyme
- ½ teaspoon mild chilli powder
- 300 g (10 oz) sweet potatoes, scrubbed and cut into small chunks
- 350 g (11½ oz) ready-cooked ham in one piece, cut into dice
- 150 g (5 oz) cranberries
- 100 ml (3½ fl oz) crème fraîche
- salt and pepper

what you do

1. Season the flour with a little salt and pepper on a plate. Cut the turkey into small chunks and coat with the seasoned flour.

2. Melt the butter in a flameproof casserole and fry the turkey for 5 minutes, or until golden on all sides. Add the onions and celery to the casserole and fry for 4–5 minutes until softened. Tip in any remaining flour left on the plate. Pour in the stock, add the thyme and chilli powder and bring to a simmer, stirring.

3. Cover the casserole and cook in a preheated oven, 180°C (350°F), Gas Mark 4, for 45 minutes.

4. Stir the sweet potatoes and ham into the casserole and return to the oven for a further 30 minutes. Stir in the cranberries and crème fraîche and season to taste with salt and pepper. Return to the oven for a final 15 minutes before serving.

Sweet Stuff and Drinks

choc chip
ice cream
sandwhiches

peach &
raspberry melba

bircher muesli

rhubarb & ginger slump

chocolate fudge brownie

syrup sponge pudding

prune clafoutis

crunchy berry brûlée

pumpkin seed & apricot muesli

baked honey peaches

passion fruit & mango mess

crunchy pear crumble

creamy chocolate pudding

banana caramel puffs

peach & raspberry melba

choc chip ice cream sandwiches

tiramisu

summer fruit gratin

hot caribbean fruit salad

cardamom coffee

lemon grass tea

tropical fruit smoothie

yogurt & berry smoothie

bircher muesli

what you need

- 200 g (7 oz) buckwheat flakes
- 300 ml (½ pint) milk
- 100 ml (3½ fl oz) apple juice
- 1 apple, peeled and grated

To serve
- 2 tablespoons clear honey
- 100 g (3½ oz) ready-to-eat dried fruit, such as mango, apricots or sultanas
- 100 g (3½ oz) hazelnuts, toasted and roughly chopped
- poached or canned fruit, such as peaches or berries

what you do

Mix together the buckwheat flakes, milk, apple juice and apple in a bowl. Cover with clingfilm and leave to soak overnight.

To serve, stir the honey, dried fruit and nuts into the muesli mixture. Spoon into serving bowls, then top with the poached or canned fruit.

STUDENT TIP

When it comes to shopping for everyday items, a quick and easy way to save money is to switch from big brands to own brands. Breakfast cereals, condiments, drinks and cleaning products are just some of the own-brand shopping-trolley staples that will slash your budget.

rhubarb & ginger slump

Cost ££ **Timing** ⏱ **Serves** 4–6

What you need

- 0 g (1½ lb) rhubarb, immed and cut into chunks
- ablespoon self-raising flour
- g (2 oz) granulated sugar
- pieces of stem ginger in rup, drained and chopped, us 2 tablespoons syrup from e jar

ping

- 5 g (3 oz) butter, softened
- 00 g (3½ oz) self-raising flour
- 5 g (3 oz) granulated sugar
- tablespoons milk
- egg, beaten

what you do

1. Place the rhubarb, flour, sugar, chopped ginger and syrup in a shallow ovenproof dish and toss together. Cover with foil and place in a preheated oven, 190°C (375°F), Gas Mark 5, for 3 minutes.
2. Meanwhile, make the topping. Place all the ingredients in a food processor and blend until smooth. Alternatively, rub the butter into the dry ingredients with your fingertips and then stir in the milk and beaten egg.
3. Uncover the rhubarb and spoon over the topping. Return to the oven for a further 25 minutes, or until the topping is golden and cooked through.

chocolate fudge brownie

what you need

- 200 g (7 oz) butter
- 200 g (7 oz) plain dark chocolate, chopped
- 175 g (6 oz) soft dark brown sugar
- 150 g (5 oz) caster sugar
- 4 eggs, beaten
- 50 g (2 oz) ground almonds
- 75 g (3 oz) plain flour
- vanilla ice cream, to serve (optional)

what you do

1. Melt the butter and chocolate in a shallow ovenproof dish, about 23 cm (9 inches) across, over a low heat. Remove from the heat and leave to cool for a couple of minutes.
2. Beat together the sugars and eggs in a bowl, then stir in the chocolate mixture followed by the almonds and flour.
3. Wipe the rim of the ovenproof dish with a damp piece of kitchen paper to neaten, then pour in the chocolate mixture. Bake in a preheated oven, 180°C (350°F), Gas Mark 4, for 25 minutes, or until just set. Serve warm with vanilla ice cream, if liked.

syrup sponge pudding

what you need

- 175 g (6 oz) butter, softened, plus extra for greasing
- 175 g (6 oz) caster sugar
- 175 g (6 oz) self-raising flour
- 1 teaspoon baking powder
- 3 eggs
- 1 teaspoon vanilla extract
- 3 tablespoons milk
- finely grated zest of ½ lemon
- 6 tablespoons golden syrup
- cream or custard, to serve

what you do

1. Grease a 1.2 litre (2 pint) pudding basin with butter. Place all the ingredients, except the golden syrup, in a food processor and blend until smooth. Spoon 4 tablespoons of the golden syrup into the bottom of the prepared pudding basin, then add the pudding mixture and smooth the surface with a knife.

2. Cover with microwave-proof clingfilm and pierce the film a couple of times with a sharp knife. Cook in a microwave oven on medium heat for about 12 minutes. Test to see if it is cooked by inserting a skewer into the pudding; it should come out clean.

3. Leave to rest for 3 minutes, then turn out on to a deep plate and spoon over the remaining golden syrup. Serve with cream or custard.

prune clafoutis

Cost
££

Timing

Serves
4

what you need

- butter, for greasing
- 3 eggs
- 125 g (4 oz) caster sugar
- 50 g (2 oz) plain flour
- 150 ml (¼ pint) double cream
- 150 ml (¼ pint) milk
- 1 teaspoon vanilla extract
- 75 g (3 oz) pitted soft prunes

what you do

Lightly grease a shallow ovenproof dish with butter. Whisk together the eggs and sugar in a bowl until pale, frothy and tripled in volume. Sift the flour into the bowl and lightly fold in. Add the cream, milk and vanilla extract and mix until just combined. Pour into the prepared ovenproof dish and bake in a preheated oven, 190°C (375°F), Gas Mark 5, for 5 minutes, or until the surface is just starting to set. Scatter over the prunes, then return to the oven for a further 15–20 minutes until the clafoutis is risen and golden.

crunchy berry brûlée

what you need

- 250 g (8 oz) mascarpone cheese
- 300 ml (½ pint) ready-made fresh custard
- 150 g (5 oz) mixed berries
- 100 g (3½ oz) caster sugar
- 1½ tablespoons water

what you do

1. Beat the mascarpone in a bowl until smooth. Gently stir in the custard. Transfer the mixture to a serving dish and scatter the berries over the top.
2. Place the sugar and measured water in a small heavy-based saucepan and slowly bring to the boil, carefully swirling the pan from time to time. Keep cooking until the sugar dissolves, then turns a deep caramel colour. Pour over the berries and leave for a few minutes to harden.

STUDENT TIP

Whether you're lucky enough to have a dishwasher in your digs or you have to get down and dirty with the dishes, always rinse pots, pans and plates as soon as they've been used. That way, if the dishwashing fairies turn up late for their shift, the food won't have dried like a layer of cement and washing up will be easier.

pumpkin seed & apricot muesli

what you need

Cost **££** Timing Serves **2**

- 50 g (2 oz) jumbo rolled oats
- 1 tablespoon sultanas or raisins
- 1 tablespoon pumpkin seeds
- 1 tablespoon chopped almonds
- 2 tablespoons chopped ready-to-eat dried apricots
- 2 tablespoons fruit juice, such as apple or orange juice, or water
- 2 small apples, peeled and grated
- 3 tablespoons milk or natural yogurt, to serve

what you do

1. Place the oats, sultanas or raisins, pumpkin seeds, almonds and apricots in a bowl with the fruit juice or water. Add the apple and mix well. Spoon into serving bowls and serve topped with milk or yogurt.

baked honey peaches

Cost **£** Timing Serves **4**

what you do

1. Grease a shallow baking dish with butter. Place the peaches, skin-side down, in the prepared baking dish. Dot the peaches with butter, then sprinkle with the almonds, drizzle with the honey and dust with a little cinnamon.
2. Bake in a preheated oven, 200°C (400°F), Gas Mark 6, for 10–15 minutes until the peaches are starting to colour and the almonds have lightly browned. Serve the peaches with the juices drizzled over, and topped with a spoonful of soured cream.

what you need

- 50 g (2 oz) butter, plus extra for greasing
- 4 large peaches, halved and stoned
- 50 g (2 oz) flaked almonds
- 75 g (3 oz) clear honey
- ground cinnamon, for dusting
- soured cream, to serve

passion fruit & mango mess

Cost
£

Timing
🕐

Serves
4

- 300 ml (½ pint) double cream
- 2-3 tablespoons icing sugar
- 4 meringue nests, crushed
- 1 mango, peeled, stoned and sliced
- 1 passion fruit, halved

what you do

1. Whip the cream with the icing sugar in a bowl until it just holds its shape.
2. Gently stir in the meringue, most of the mango and a little of the passion fruit pulp. Spoon into glasses and top with the remaining fruit.

Variation

For a passion fruit and mango cream, peel, stone and chop 1 mango and divide among 4 glasses. Whisk 1 egg yolk with 2 tablespoons caster sugar in a bowl until very frothy and pale, then stir in the pulp of 2 passion fruit. Whip 200 ml (7 fl oz) double cream in a separate bowl until soft peaks form, then stir into the egg mixture and whisk until thickened. Gently stir in 1 tablespoon orange liqueur and 75 g (3 oz) crushed meringues. Spoon over the mango and top with a little more chopped fruit, if liked.

crunchy pear crumble

what you need

Cost
£

Timing

Serves
6

- 6 pears, peeled, cored and chopped
- 2 tablespoons soft light brown sugar
- ½ teaspoon ground cinnamon
- 4 tablespoons water
- custard, to serve

Topping
- 75 g (3 oz) soft light brown sugar
- ½ teaspoon ground cinnamon
- 125 g (4 oz) rolled oats
- 75 g (3 oz) plain flour
- 75 g (3 oz) butter
- 1 tablespoon golden syrup

what you do

1. Place the pears in a shallow ovenproof dish with the sugar, cinnamon and measured water and stir together. Cover with foil and place in a preheated oven, 190°C (375°F), Gas Mark 5, for 5 minutes.
2. Meanwhile, make the crumble topping. Place the sugar in a food processor with the cinnamon, oats, flour and butter and pulse until the mixture resembles fine breadcrumbs. Alternatively, rub the butter into the dry ingredients with your fingertips. Stir the golden syrup into the topping mixture.
3. Remove the pears from the oven, uncover and scatter the topping over them. Return to the oven for a further 20–25 minutes until bubbling and lightly browned. Serve warm with custard.

creamy chocolate pudding

Cost
£

Timing

Serves
4

what you need

- 75 g (3 oz) granulated sugar
- 3 tablespoons cornflour
- 25 g (1 oz) cocoa powder
- 3 eggs
- 500 ml (17 fl oz) milk
- 75 g (3 oz) milk chocolate, chopped

To serve
- whipped cream
- grated milk chocolate

what you do

1. Place the sugar, cornflour and cocoa powder in a heatproof bowl and whisk in the eggs. Bring the milk to the boil in a saucepan, then whisk a little of it into the egg mixture. Transfer the cocoa mixture to the saucepan, stir well and cook for 3–5 minutes, stirring continuously, until thickened.

2. Place the chopped chocolate in the bowl, sieve the chocolate custard on top and stir until smooth. Cover the surface with clingfilm to prevent a skin forming, then place in the freezer for 15 minutes, stirring occasionally, until cool.

3. When the chocolate custard is cool, divide among serving bowls, top with whipped cream and sprinkle with grated chocolate.

Variation

For creamy chocolate truffles, bring 75 ml (3 fl oz) double cream to the boil in a small heavy-based saucepan. Place 150 g (5 oz) chopped plain dark chocolate in a heatproof bowl with 25 g (1 oz) butter. Pour over the cream and stir until smooth. Place in the freezer for 15 minutes, stirring occasionally, until the mixture has set. Use a teaspoon to scoop out pieces of the mixture, form into balls and roll in cocoa powder to serve.

banana caramel puffs

Cost
££

Timing
⏱ ⏱

Serves
4

what you need

- 150 g (5 oz) soft light brown sugar
- 50 ml (2 fl oz) water
- 25 g (1 oz) butter
- 300 g (10 oz) ready-rolled puff pastry
- 2 bananas, sliced

Variation
For banana and caramel pots, slice 2 bananas and divide among serving bowls. Whip 150 ml (¼ pint) double cream in a bowl until soft peaks form, then stir in 1 tablespoon dulce de leche or other caramel sauce. Spoon over the banana, then drizzle with more dulce de leche and top with chopped pecans.

what you do

1. Heat the sugar and measured water in a large ovenproof frying pan until golden and caramel coloured. Carefully add the butter and swirl around the pan until melted.
2. Meanwhile, cut out 4 rounds from the pastry using a 7 cm (3 inch) cookie cutter or glass.
3. Carefully arrange the banana slices in 4 circles in the caramel, then place a pastry round on top of each. Place in a preheated oven, 220°C (425°F), Gas Mark 7, for 15 minutes, or until the pastry is puffed and cooked through. Use a spatula to turn out of the pan and drizzle with the remaining sauce.

peach & aspberry melba

- 250 ml (8 fl oz) water
- 125 g (4 oz) caster sugar
- 1 teaspoon vanilla extract
- 4 peaches, halved and stoned
- 8 scoops of vanilla ice cream
- 125 g (4 oz) raspberries
- biscuit curls, to serve

what you do

1. Place the measured water, sugar and vanilla extract in a saucepan, and cook over a low heat until the sugar dissolves, then cook over a high heat for 5–10 minutes until syrupy.
2. Add the peach halves and cook for a further 5 minutes, or until tender, then leave to cool. Remove the skins and thinly slice the peaches.
3. Arrange the peach slices, ice cream and half the raspberries in sundae glasses. Press the remaining raspberries through a sieve set over a bowl to make a coulis. Drizzle the coulis over the top of the sundaes and serve with biscuit curls.

choc chip ice cream sandwiches

Cost
££

Timing
◐ ◐

Serves
4

what you do

what you need

- 150 g (5 oz) butter, softened
- 100 g (3½ oz) granulated sugar
- 100 g (3½ oz) soft light brown sugar
- 1 egg, beaten
- 175 g (6 oz) plain flour
- 1 teaspoon baking powder
- 1 teaspoon vanilla extract
- 100 g (3½ oz) mixed plain dark, milk and white chocolate chips
- 4 scoops of vanilla ice cream

1. Line a baking sheet with greaseproof paper. Beat the butter and sugars together in a bowl until light and fluffy, then stir in the egg. Beat in the flour, baking powder and vanilla extract, then stir in three-quarters of the chocolate chips.

2. Use a teaspoon to dollop 24 walnut-sized balls of dough, well spaced apart, on to the prepared baking sheet and flatten gently. Scatter with the remaining chocolate chips and cook in the preheated oven, 190°C (375°F), Gas Mark 5, for 8–10 minutes until golden and just cooked through.

3. Leave the cookies to cool on a wire rack, then serve 2 cookies to each person, sandwiched together with a scoop of vanilla ice cream.

tiramisu

Cost
£££

Timing

Serves
4

what you need

- 200 ml (7 fl oz) double cream
- 50 ml (2 fl oz) Marsala wine
- 250 g (8 oz) mascarpone cheese
- 4 tablespoons icing sugar
- 1 teaspoon vanilla extract
- 300 ml (½ pint) very strong coffee, cooled
- 20 sponge fingers
- 25 g (1 oz) plain dark chocolate, grated, to decorate

what you do

1. Whip the cream in a bowl until stiff peaks form. Reserve 1 tablespoon of the Marsala, then stir the remaining Marsala into the cream with the mascarpone, 3 tablespoons of the icing sugar and the vanilla extract.
2. Stir the remaining Marsala and icing sugar into the coffee, then dip 4 of the sponge fingers into the mixture and place each in the bottom of a glass or small serving dish. The sponge fingers should be just soft, not soggy.
3. Spoon some of the creamy mixture on top, then repeat the layers to use up the remaining ingredients. Chill in the fridge for 20 minutes, then serve sprinkled with grated chocolate.

STUDENT TIP

Stick to use-by dates.

Food poisoning is a daily danger for students preparing food in less than salubrious surroundings. Lower your chances by sticking to the advice on food labels — if its use-by date is today, don't let it fester in the fridge for another couple of nights.

summer fruit gratin

- 2 peaches, halved, stoned and sliced
- 4 red plums, halved, stoned and sliced
- 150 g (5 oz) mixed raspberries and blackberries (or all raspberries)

- 200 g (7 oz) mascarpone cheese
- 4 tablespoons caster sugar
- 2 tablespoons double cream
- grated zest of 1 lime

what you do

1. Arrange all the fruit in a shallow ovenproof dish. Mix the mascarpone in a bowl with 2 tablespoons of the sugar, the cream and lime zest, then spoon over the fruit and spread into an even layer. Sprinkle the top with the remaining sugar.
2. Place the ovenproof dish on a baking sheet and bake in a preheated oven, 190°C (375°F), Gas Mark 5, for 15 minutes, or until the cheese has softened and the sugar topping has caramelized. Serve immediately.

hot caribbean fruit salad

Cost
££

Timing

Serves
4–5

what you need

- 50 g (2 oz) unsalted butter
- 50 g (2 oz) light muscovado sugar
- 1 large papaya, halved, deseeded, peeled and sliced
- 1 large mango, peeled, stoned and sliced
- ½ pineapple, skinned, cored and cut into chunks
- 400 ml (14 fl oz) can coconut milk
- grated zest and juice of 1 lime

Variation

For baked nectarines with orange meringues, add the finely grated rind of 1 orange to the meringue mixture with the cornflour. Cut 2 peeled and stoned nectarines into thin slices and place in an ovenproof dish. Sprinkle with 2 tablespoons sugar and 1 tablespoon orange juice, then bake for 45 minutes with the meringues. Serve the fruit over the meringues.

1. Melt the butter in a large frying pan, add the sugar and heat gently until just dissolved. Add all the fruit and cook for 2 minutes, then pour in the coconut milk and lime juice and add half the lime zest. Heat gently for 4–5 minutes, then serve warm in shallow serving bowls, sprinkled with the remaining lime zest.

cardamom coffee

what you need

- 3 tablespoons strong, freshly ground coffee (South Indian, Colombian or Javan)
- 1 teaspoon crushed cardamom seeds
- 250 ml (8 fl oz) milk
- 2 tablespoons sugar
- 600 ml (1 pint) water

what you do

1. Place the coffee, cardamom seeds, milk, sugar and measured water in a large saucepan and bring to the boil. Reduce the heat and simmer for 1–2 minutes.
2. Using a very fine-meshed sieve lined with muslin, strain the coffee into mugs and serve hot.

lemon grass tea

what you need

- 3–4 lemon grass stalks, finely chopped
- 4 teaspoons Indian tea leaves (Darjeeling or Assam)
- 750 ml (1¼ pints) water

To serve
- milk
- sugar

what you do

1. Put the lemon grass and tea leaves in a large saucepan with the measured water and bring to the boil. Reduce the heat and simmer, uncovered, for 2–3 minutes.
2. Using a very fine-meshed sieve lined with muslin, strain the tea into mugs and serve hot, adding milk and sugar to taste.

tropical fruit smoothie

what you need

Cost ££   **Timing** ◐   **Serves** 4

- 1 mango, peeled, stoned and chopped
- 2 kiwifruits, peeled and chopped
- 1 banana, cut into chunks
- 425 g (14 oz) can pineapple chunks or pieces in natural juice
- 450 ml (¾ pint) orange or apple juice
- handful of ice cubes.

what you do

1. Place all the ingredients in a food processor or blender and blitz until smooth. Pour into 4 glasses and serve immediately.

yogurt & berry smoothie

what you need

Cost ££   **Timing** ◐   **Serves** 4

- 300 ml (½ pint) natural yogurt
- 500 g (1 lb) fresh or frozen mixed summer berries, defrosted if frozen, plus extra to decorate
- 4 tablespoons millet flakes
- 3 tablespoons clear honey
- 300 ml (½ pint) cranberry juice

what you do

1. Place all the ingredients in a food processor or a blender and blitz until smooth. Pour into 4 glasses, decorate with a few extra whole berries and serve immediately.

Index

Picture Credits
123RF akulamatiau 10; Baloncici 11a; hamik 11bl; Joshua Resnick 11br; Victoria Shibut 2; Yulia Davidovich 12.
Octopus Publishing Group 58r; David Munns 138; Emma Neish 94; Ian Garlick 133; Ian Wallace 41, 54, 74, 82, 85, 93; Lis Parsons 16, 20, 30, 39, 45, 49, 50, 60, 67, 111, 125; Stephen Conroy 24, 47, 62, 64, 73, 76, 78, 79, 87, 115, 117, 118, 127, 134, 140, 141, 145; Will Heap 33, 37, 40, 42, 43, 77, 81, 86, 95, 98, 99, 100, 101, 102, 110, 131, 168, 169; William Reavell 126, 128, 129; William Shaw 1, 17, 19, 22, 26, 28, 29, 35, 36, 44, 46, 48, 51, 52, 53, 56, 57, 61, 65, 66, 69, 70, 71, 80, 83, 88, 89, 90, 96, 97, 107, 108, 112, 116, 119, 120, 121, 123, 124, 130, 143, 144, 146, 151, 152, 153, 154, 155, 156, 159, 160, 161, 163, 164, 165, 167.

Additional picture credits:
Shutterstock inxti; Alenka Karabanova; natrot; Picsfive; Piotr pabijan; STILLFX.